Competence and Self-Care in Counselling and Psychotherapy

D1600435

What is it that makes a counsellor or psychotherapist competent?

In *Competence and Self-Care in Counselling and Psychotherapy*, Gerrie Hughes offers a framework for understanding what being competent means for individual practitioners, both generally and in moment-by-moment work with clients. Divided into two sections, Part I, 'The competent self', and Part II, 'Care of the self', the book explores care and replenishment of the self as an essential requirement for maintaining competence.

The Competence Framework presented here suggests that the three elements of Practitioner, Client and Context are essential factors for making good therapeutic choices, as well as offering a structure for reflection, either individually or in supervision. The eight principles that elaborate on these elements provide a route to explore competence that is relevant for any theoretical orientation and appropriate for practitioners at any stage. The reader is encouraged to make their own exploration of a number of factors that influence competence and to identify development of the self as both a necessary preparation for therapeutic work and as a continuing outcome of being a therapist. In addition, Hughes emphasizes the importance of having a sound ethical framework and utilizing professional structures as well as examining the contribution of supervision to the development and maintenance of competence.

This book is an ideal choice for counsellors, psychotherapists, supervisors and trainers who wish to maintain a robust standard of practice and for those employing them.

Gerrie Hughes has a private practice in Cardiff and writes both fiction and non-fiction. She trained in Gestalt psychotherapy after leaving her first career with British Gas. She has more than twenty years' experience as a therapist, supervisor and trainer and has worked in the NHS, in education and in a number of training institutes.

Competence and Self-Care in Counselling and Psychotherapy

Gerrie Hughes

Routledge
Taylor & Francis Group

LONDON AND NEW YORK

First published 2014
by Routledge
27 Church Road, Hove, East Sussex, BN3 2FA

and by Routledge
711 Third Avenue, New York, NY 10017

Routledge is an imprint of the Taylor & Francis Group, an informa business

British Library Cataloguing in Publication Data
A catalogue record for this book is available from the British Library

Library of Congress Cataloging in Publication Data
Hughes, Gerrie.
Competence and self-care in counselling and psychotherapy/Gerrie Hughes.
—First Edition.
pages cm
1. Counseling—Moral and ethical aspects. 2. Psychotherapy—Moral
and ethical aspects. I. Title.
BF636.67.H84 2014
158.3—dc23
2013034459

ISBN: 978-0-415-82806-2 (hbk)
ISBN: 978-0-415-82807-9 (pbk)
ISBN: 978-1-315-81440-7 (ebk)

Typeset in Times
by Book Now Ltd, London

Printed and bound in the United States of America by Publishers Graphics,
LLC on sustainably sourced paper.

Contents

Acknowledgements

My thanks to Kate Bowman, Keith Hackwood, Susan Sutherland and colleagues at BCPC for your support. Special thanks to Linda Ford for your help and encouragement.

Introduction

Counsellors and psychotherapists, in the main, do their jobs with sincerity and compassion. There are many benefits: being involved in a worthwhile endeavour that makes a real difference for people; encouragement to be concerned with their own personal and professional development, and a sense of belonging to a profession that is gaining recognition as it continues to evolve. There are also risks. Having continually to be open to deep distress, available for connection with one person after another, and working alone, relying solely on their own resources to support them, can gradually deplete practitioners. This book is about how to maximize the benefits and deal with the risks, so that the experience of both practitioners and clients is enhanced.

Being human, and vulnerable, and flawed, practitioners misunderstand, react inappropriately and make mistakes. While this can often be therapeutic for clients – if the aftermath is handled sensitively – it leaves practitioners with a question. Is this difficulty the natural consequence of two human beings meeting together as authentically as they can, or is there some deficit that could be made good? Possible answers to that important question are offered in the following chapters.

I did not set about writing this from a place of unassailable competence, but from the position of a practitioner who has to deal with day-to-day challenges as best I can. When I fail, as I often do, I appreciate the support I receive from supervisors and colleagues as I try to learn what lessons I can from the situation. It is important that, as a profession, we accept that each of us has limitations, and ensure that there are structures in place for when things go wrong.

Each of us is different, so every individual would have her or his own way of being competent. The book is structured so that readers can identify what being competent means for them, regardless of the orientation of their training and length of time in practice. While I use examples from two prominent UK professional associations, the British Association for Counselling and Psychotherapy (BACP) and the United Kingdom Council for Psychotherapy (UKCP), I am aware that other associations, both here and abroad, have their own codes of ethics and procedures. My intention throughout the book is to acknowledge that readers have different experiences of: accrediting bodies; training providers and work contexts. My invitation is that practitioners heighten awareness of how their own individual experiences shape their potential to be competent.

Competence is not a condition that once achieved is always there, like accreditation. Neither has it to do with lists of competences that measure minimum requirements expected to be met by people in certain roles. Competence is about how we make moment-by-moment choices in our work. It is individual and contextual.

The book is structured in this way:

Part I: The competent self

Chapter 1 explores the difference between effectiveness – getting something right, and competence, which is about background, training and being embedded in professional structures. Those structures include supervision and being bound by the ethical codes of professional associations.

Chapter 2 discusses how competence can be defined and introduces the **Competence Framework**, a simple structure for exploring matters of competence, using the three elements of **Practitioner**, **Client** and **Context**. The three elements are the basis of a series of eight **Principles**, each of which is more fully explored in the following chapters.

Chapter 3 is the first of four chapters dedicated to the **Practitioner** element of the Framework. A brief re-visiting of psychoanalytic theories, particularly those of child-development, is meant to encourage readers to explore their own early experience. Understanding the development of the self is an important contribution towards being able to define competence for an individual practitioner.

Chapter 4 discusses matters of difference and diversity. Readers are invited to consider how their own gender, culture, physical ability or disability, sexuality, class, age and belief system define them as a person and as a professional.

Chapter 5 focuses on how potential students choose the training course they wish to undertake, and demonstrates that training courses equip their graduates in different ways. The experience of different practitioners is offered as an illustration.

Chapter 6 looks at the experience of being a therapist. Factors that may either facilitate competent practice, or potentially undermine it are identified and discussed, and the contribution that the requirement for Continuing Professional Development makes to competence is examined. The impact being a therapist has on personal life and, the influence of current life experiences on therapy are also explored.

Chapter 7 is concerned with the **Client** element of the **Competence Framework**. It may be difficult for an individual practitioner to work competently with certain clients. While this is a natural, and perhaps inevitable limitation, understanding why this may be the case, and having strategies in place for when it occurs, are supportive for both practitioner and client.

Chapter 8 identifies how **Context**, the third element of the **Competence Framework** influences practice. Context includes the organizational setting, physical location, ethical framework, policies and procedures, and arrangements for supervision.

Part II: Care of the self

Chapter 9 is devoted to identifying when difficulties may be occurring and suggests some possible remedies: an exploration of professional self-care.

Chapter 10 is dedicated to supervision. It begins with an exploration of Casement's 'Internal Supervisor' and shows how it can be used to maintain competent practice. The contribution of reflective practice in recognizing and developing competence is acknowledged. Supervisors may help supervisees who are students to develop an internal supervisor, or observer self, so that they can use it for measuring their own competence in day-to-day practice. There are discussions of how supervisors can support all their supervisees to understand their levels of competence, and to be able to acknowledge when they are breached.

Chapter 11 acknowledges the need of replenishment for the self that is so fundamentally involved in therapeutic work. Care for body and environment, creativity and spirituality are discussed.

Each of the chapters includes activities that can be undertaken individually, in supervision or by a group. My invitation is that you use the book as a basis for exploration of what being competent, and taking care of your self, means for you.

Part I

The competent self

Chapter 1

What do we mean when we talk about competence?

Chapter outline

The concepts of competence and effectiveness are introduced and the differences between them in the context of counselling and psychotherapy are discussed. The significance of self-care for maintaining competence is outlined, emphasizing how therapeutic work can make specific demands on practitioners. A foundation is laid for an ongoing exploration of the impact of issues of diversity. The essential role of supervision in the maintenance of competence is acknowledged, together with a recognition of the significance of codes of ethics.

Can competence be defined?

Competence is contextual: a practitioner may be competent with a particular client in a particular situation and not competent in another. It can change from moment to moment as we negotiate the demands of client work. Because counsellors and psychotherapists are human beings, we are subject to limitations. This brings vulnerability, but it is also our great strength. We could not meet our clients in their vulnerability if we were not acquainted with our own.

A sense of being competent, or not, can often be subjective: I feel that I am working competently as I sit with a client. Another time I might feel that I have definitely strayed out of my area of competence and be wondering desperately what to do about it! I am certain that there also many times I step outside my competence levels and remain unaware that I have done so.

Many different elements contribute to defining competence. Tim Bond's definition states:

> Professional competence requires having adequate skills, being properly qualified and trained, effective and working ethically.
>
> (2010: 120)

While this does not appear contentious, it leaves open to question what 'adequate' skills might look like. This would depend on what a practitioner has been trained in, and is qualified to do, and how effectiveness is recognized and measured within that approach. Each practitioner would need to arrive at the answers to these questions individually based on: their background and training; the client group with whom they work and the context in which it takes place. These elements will be explored in more detail in subsequent chapters.

Competence and effectiveness

Sometimes the terms competence and effectiveness can be used interchangeably. It is helpful to define how they are different, because doing so can allow the meaning of each of them to be more clearly understood. Here are some commonly held definitions:

Competence:
Ability
The state of being legally qualified
Language knowledge

Effectiveness:
Producing results
Producing a favourable impression
Ready for action

For the purposes of this book I will use the word competence to mean that a practitioner:

- has had, or is in the process of pursuing, an appropriate training;
- meets any criteria that may be required;
- understands and uses 'the language': knows the technical terms and styles of communicating;
- is embedded in structures that accredit, support, set ethical boundaries and censure when necessary.

Effectiveness is about producing a successful outcome. In a therapy context a successful outcome might be:

- the maintenance of a solid working relationship (Clarkson, 1995);
- changes to a client's sense of themselves and/or the way they engage with the world (and/or the therapist) (Rogers, 1967).

Therapy is concerned with the nature of the relationship between individuals, so any person may be effective in providing many of the conditions that define a therapeutic encounter, without having done specific training (Berman and Norton (1985) in Rowan (2005)). This being the case, it is important to recognize that what makes counselling and psychotherapy into a profession, and distinguishes it from the helpful listening and confidences exchanged between friends, is the structure provided by the existence of:

- a well-tested theoretical base;
- properly evaluated training courses;
- respected accrediting organizations;
- sound ethical principles;
- the application of sanctions.

Competence is established by the evaluation procedures of training organizations, and in adhering to the requirements of professional associations such as BACP and UKCP. Effectiveness is measured by growth and change in our clients, underpinned by the findings of an increasing number of research projects and the growing acceptance of psychological therapies by other professions and the public in general.

The nature of therapeutic work means that it may be possible for a practitioner to be competent, and still not effective in a particular situation. This is because of the myriad of factors that influence an encounter between individuals. Yalom writes:

> Though the public may believe that therapists guide patients systematically and sure-handedly through predictable stages of therapy to a foreknown goal this is rarely the case: instead … therapists wobble, improvise and grope for direction.
>
> (1991: 13)

The scope of this book involves an exploration of both competence and effectiveness, and the relationship between them.

Self-care as essential element of maintaining competence

While the professional structures described in the previous section are crucial to establishing an individual's competence, there is another factor that is equally significant. This is the psychological, emotional, physical and spiritual robustness of the practitioner. All of us have limitations, no matter how highly trained and extensively experienced we are. It is also the case that our flaws and imperfections are part of what make us effective in our work with others.

Research into therapists' feelings of being incompetent carried out by Thierault and Gazzola identified that:

> The practice of psychotherapy can be a hazardous undertaking (Brady, Healy, Norcross, & Guy, 1995) with almost three quarters of therapists reporting some level of role-related personal distress (Guy, Poelstra, & Stark, 1989). Among the elements that contribute to therapist distress, feelings of incompetence (FOI) figure markedly. Feelings of incompetence (FOI) refer to a therapist's belief that his or her ability, judgment, and/or effectiveness as a therapist is absent, reduced, or challenged internally (Thierault & Gazzola, 2005). The literature that examines topics such as the therapist's experience of therapy, therapist self-care, and the hazards of practicing as a psychotherapist is peppered with allusions to FOI (Daniels, 1974; Deutsch, 1984; Farber & Heifetz, 1982; Guy, 2000; Mahoney, 1991; Mearns, 1990).
>
> (2008: 20)

As practitioners, each of us will decide whether our own subjective experience is similar or different to that described here. While it is beyond the scope of the research to identify the causes of these feelings of incompetence when they arise, or to validate whether they are objectively 'true' or not, we may be interested to explore this for ourselves, if we do experience similar feelings. For myself, I definitely experience feelings of incompetence on a regular basis. I believe there are a number of possible causes:

- The situation is actually one in which I cannot work competently or effectively, for whatever reason.
- I am experiencing a period of therapeutic 'not knowing'. The heuristic nature of therapeutic work means that we (client and therapist)

need to make powerful contact with feelings of not knowing what is going on, or how to progress, before something new can arise in the space.

- I am responding to something my client is communicating word-lessly, sometimes called counter-transference.
- I am overloaded, exhausted, ill or approaching burnout.

Because therapeutic work is rarely straightforward, often a mixture of these underlying causes may be present. Relying in part on our own vulnerability to be able to work effectively means that sometimes we think of ourselves as 'wounded healers'. This term is often associated with Carl Jung, although it has connections back to Greek classical mythology. Jung's understanding is that limitations are certainly natural and inevitable, and may even be desirable (Sedgwick, 2004). While identification with the wounded healer archetype may make sense for some practitioners, it will not fit for everybody. The assumption that we all have limitations and will eventually encounter situations in which we cannot work competently, is not meant to undermine practitioners, but to be supportive, especially because feelings of incompetence have been recognized as an issue for therapists.

Individuals naturally differ for many reasons, although personal histories and the choice of theoretical orientation (which probably inform one another) may be significant contributing factors. If it were to be generally recognized that many practitioners do feel that their sense of being competent is challenged from time to time, then structures could be put in place to deal with issues when they arise, which is likely to maintain and enhance the high standard of practice to which professionals aspire.

As therapists, we use the 'self' as the means of engaging with our clients in a meaningful way. Orientations might differ in their emphasis, but work with clients has, by its nature, a way of forcing practitioners to look at our selves and our own responses, encouraging us to develop and change as a consequence. For me, this is what keeps it being fascinating in the longer term.

It can be difficult to identify a distinct line between personal and professional development. Each is connected with both the topics of this book. Personal development, the maintenance of professional competence and the care of the self all have their roots in the needs of a person with a body, a mind, emotions, and a spiritual aspect that might look very individual, living and working within a particular context.

Diversity and competence

Each of us is unique. As human beings we have many similarities, and also many areas of difference. Some differences are accepted as having a particular significance. These are:

- ethnicity
- culture
- gender
- sexual orientation
- class
- religion and spirituality
- physical and mental ability or disability
- age.

This list is in random order and is probably not exhaustive.

In some circumstances, we cannot really know what it is like to be 'other'. Several years ago I was one of a minority of women in a training situation. The male tutor asked me how women might think differently from men about the issues under discussion. I thought for a moment, then responded that I wasn't able to answer because, while I might be able to have a sense of how women generically might react, I had no idea of how men would. The tutor knew his perspective would be limited, but somehow thought mine would be less so. This situation highlights an aspect of the discussion of diversity, which can sometimes assume a default: often male, western, heterosexual, able-bodied and middle class. Those of us who do not fit those categories carry the identification of being the 'different' ones.

Sometimes there is a possibility of seeing the world from a different point of view. While we probably do not know exactly what it is like to be a member of a different ethnic group, some of us will have had the experience of being part of a minority in a larger population. In our thirties, we cannot really know what it is like to be in our seventies although, conversely, we can in our seventies remember what it was like to be thirty (for ourselves as individuals, and in so far as we are remembering accurately).

Awareness of difference is important, but it is also problematic, because so many of our attitudes and assumptions about it are inevitably out-of-awareness (Wheeler, 2006). When I suffered a temporary condition that meant that I had to use a walking-stick, I was astonished by how differently I was treated in public situations. I was ignored in shops, and found that passers-by would either patronize me, or else hurry past me as fast as they could, so as not to be held up. I began to understand the fear that the able-bodied can have of those with visible disabilities. It is understandable because, at a primitive level, physical vulnerability exposes an individual to greater danger and consequent possibility of death, which in turn endangers anyone connected with that person. The fact that my attitude had been similar to the people I felt were treating me in a discriminatory way was a challenging discovery for me! It was as if, until I had become physically vulnerable myself, and experienced the reaction of others to me, I could not bring my own attitude to individuals with physical issues into awareness.

Practitioners from minority ethnic groups are starting to have more of a voice in the profession, and are speaking about how cultural expectations influence the therapeutic relationship and framework. There are still so few people involved though, that it can feel to members of minority groups like an enormous burden that is disproportionately held. Issues of power are relevant here, with Western culture still having a high degree of dominance in the world, although that is changing (Littlewood and Lipsedge, 1989).

Power differentials can also be significant for other areas of difference: sexuality, gender, class, age, physical ability and degree of mental health. Mental health is a particularly sensitive area for therapy, because it is where we see ourselves being effective, but also where, in some situations, the limits to our effectiveness can become apparent (D'Ardenne and Mahtani, 1999; Davies and Neal, 1996; Kareem and Littlewood 2000).

Sensitivity to different beliefs, assumptions and ways of being in the world is a significant issue for practitioners as we go about our work. Profound difference can be one of the ways in which we come unstuck with our clients, and can underlie the ways we alienate and disempower our selves. Chapter 4 explores issues of diversity.

Competence and supervision

Probably the most natural context within which competence and care for the self can be explored is that of supervision. While it is important to reflect individually on what competence means for each of us, and to what extent we are competent and effective in our practice, it is important to have a perspective from other practitioners too. Supervisors know our selves and our work, and the regular supervisory meeting offers a space for a dialogue.

It is usual to bring difficulties with clients to supervision. Encountering difficulties does not necessarily mean that we have moved beyond our limits of competence. Therapeutic work is hard, demanding for both participants and moves at its own pace. Supervisory support helps us to withstand the vicissitudes involved.

Sometimes issues brought to supervision can indicate limits to competence. For example: a practitioner who has personally experienced only short-term therapy may find difficulty working in a long-term way with their clients; a client may bring an issue that is unusual and may not have been covered by a general training; the client may parallel something unresolved in the therapist's past or current circumstances. Practitioners can find it difficult to acknowledge limitations, particularly earlier on in their career. This is one of the reasons it is important to create a climate that accepts limitations as a matter of course. Supervisors can contribute greatly to this by being open about their own limitations, and modelling acceptance of them. Hawkins and Shohet remind us that:

> What most supervisees forget, or do not even consider, is that supervisors may also be anxious about how they are being judged or evaluated by their supervisees. Evaluation and review should be a two-way process and needs to be regularly scheduled into the supervision arrangements.
>
> (2006: 35)

If limitations are openly discussed and routinely accepted, then measures can be taken to address the difficulties. These could include:

- re-entering personal therapy;
- undertaking additional training;
- referring clients elsewhere.

Rather than feeling exposed and ashamed, practitioners can enjoy the warm support of their supervisor while they take advantage of the opportunity for self-development afforded by the encountering of a limitation. In Part II, Chapter 10 'Highlighting supervision' focuses on issues related to supervision in greater detail. Remedies for situations where competence is exceeded are discussed more fully in Chapter 9, 'Highlighting professional self-care'.

Competence and codes of ethics

A Code of Ethics is a significant support. It can help us identify what being competent might entail. It also offers both a structure for reflection when important decisions have to be made, and a reminder of areas that might need to be considered when we feel uneasy. The different national counselling and psychotherapy associations have their own codes of ethics. Bond (2010: 58–60) presents a useful comparison of them. Codes of ethics are easily available on the websites of the various associations.

ACCESSING CODES OF ETHICS

BACP   www.bacp.co.uk/ethical_framework/
UKCP   www.psychotherapy.org.uk/code_of_ethics.html
BPS   www.bps.org.uk/what-we-do/ethics-standards/ethics-standards

---

The following case study shows how an ethical framework can be used when a practitioner feels they have stepped outside their area of competence. Incidentally, it demonstrates how stepping outside our areas of competence can mean we are also faced with ethical dilemmas. The BACP Ethical Framework (2010) emphasizes the importance of being competent for the ability to work ethically.

CASE STUDY 1.1

Brian was a student on a counselling training, who was undertaking a voluntary placement in a local agency as part of his course. At supervision he discussed one of his clients who had disclosed to him that she had broken some of the terms of a court order that had been placed on her. His supervisor suggested they looked together at the BACP Ethical Framework as a way of exploring the possible implications of the disclosure.

After some discussion they decided together that the client had exercised her *autonomy* by taking the action she had. The disclosure was a probable consequence of the *trustworthiness* she identified with Brian. There was likely to be no danger to the client or others as a result, so the principle of *non-maleficence* was addressed. While recognizing that there had been a breach of a legal requirement, the likely

(Continued)

(Continued)

consequences of taking action would cause a rupture in the therapy that would be disproportionate. On balance it was felt that *justice* would be best served by taking no action outside the therapy room. While Brian was demonstrating his *beneficence* towards his client by bringing his concerns to supervision, his supervisor pointed out that the principle of *self-respect* implies that he was due the same amount of respect from his client that he was according to her. The supervisor wondered about the client's motives for telling Brian. Was the client looking for permission, or complicity in some way? The discussion moved towards exploring how Brian might work therapeutically with his client in future sessions.

Reflection points

What may have underlain the supervisor's curiosity about the client's motivation for telling Brian?
Are her 'wonderings' appropriate and/or ethical?
Identify some options Brian might take in going forward with the work.

Competence and what is momentarily out of awareness/the unconscious

Possibly one of the significant differences between modalities is whether they emphasize conscious or unconscious processes. As a Gestaltist, I have a whole conceptual framework for working with awareness (Wheeler, 1998), although I often find my clients uncovering material that was previously out of awareness as we explore together. Practitioners from a Cognitive Behavioural perspective could assume they are working with conscious processes. Those with a Person Centred background would probably consider themselves to be demonstrating empathy for both conscious and unconscious processes. Analysts, psychodynamic and many integrative practitioners would probably consider themselves to be working mainly with what is unconscious. Whatever approach a therapist uses, I believe that each of us has times when we are not working competently (or effectively) and are not aware of it. As the relevant issues are developed over each chapter, I will be both highlighting what can easily be known, and indicating how what is not currently known can be tracked down.

Chapter summary

The groundwork is laid for a deeper exploration of both competence and effectiveness in the following chapters, and of care for the self in Part II of the book. Readers are signposted towards the relevance of certain factors for the unfolding of the discussion. These are:

- issues of diversity and difference;
- supervision;
- codes of ethics;
- working with both what is known, and what may be as yet unknown (unconscious) but able to be brought into awareness.

ACTIVITIES

Individual reflection

1.1 You are probably familiar with what competence might look like for the modality in which you trained. If you are still in training, you will probably be even more aware of how the standard you are expected to achieve is measured. Identify three to five elements that are particularly meaningful for you in your practice and make a note of them.

1.2 You may know of other modalities. Would competence look the same for a practitioner of those modalities as it would for your own? Note down any similarities and differences you observe. If you are not familiar with another modality then you may like to look at a book that describes a range of approaches – the handbook *Individual Therapy* edited by Windy Dryden, is an example (Dryden, 1991), or talk to other practitioners with different backgrounds.

In supervision

1.3 Take the notes you made from the previous activities to your next supervision session. Your supervisor will probably be happy to discuss what you discovered. This exercise may be particularly rewarding if you and your supervisor come from different modalities.

(Continued)

(Continued)

Group activity

1.4   The facilitator leads the group into a reflective space (relax, maybe eyes closed, maybe tune into breath for a moment). Ask participants to remember a time when they felt particularly incompetent (whatever that word might mean for them); to notice what happens in their bodies as they do so. Then ask them to remember a time they felt particularly competent and notice what happens in their bodies. After a few moments ask participants to discuss their experience in pairs for a few moments initially, then in the full group.

PERSONAL REFLECTION

The activities outlined in 1.1 and 1.2 above echo some of the methods I used to approach writing this book. With my training in Gestalt, the way I conceptualized what working competently would be for me, was to consider the quality of the relationship between the client and myself and the clarity with which I can connect with my own body processes, emotions, intuitions and thoughts. Thinking comes quite a way down the list because the founders, especially Fritz Perls, valued the intellect less than the more visceral ways that human beings have to connect with each other and the world (Perls, Hefferline and Goodman, 1951). In my training, authenticity, spontaneity and creativity were prized. I felt that being a 'good gestaltist' involved the ability to dance, sing, act, tell stories, make art, and to play generally. With a client in a therapy context all this would help me to be available to engage in a way that the German philosopher Martin Büber would call I-Thou (1958/1984). It would also help me to design experiments (Zinker, 1978). The best known type of experiment is two-chair work, where a person moves from seat to seat in order portray and perhaps resolve an internal conflict, although there are potentially as many experiments as the creativity of practitioners will allow. Students training in Gestalt today may have some similar experiences to mine, although there is likely to be a far greater emphasis on academic rigour, because that is required in these more regulated times.

Chapter 2

How do we define competence?

Chapter outline

Criteria for defining competence are identified, and there is a discussion of standards for accreditation and regulation. As particular landmarks, these are differentiated from the continuous appraisal of competence that is characteristic of therapeutic work. Practitioner, Client and Context are introduced as elements of a framework for identifying principles that practitioners can use to understand the nature of their competence, and in ongoing consideration of their work with clients.

When competence is defined

Training and ongoing professional development

Practitioners have very different notions about what a definition of competence might entail. For some a checklist of skills may be a desirable model, others may consider it reductionist to be so concrete about such a nebulous and nuanced undertaking. It is likely that the theoretical orientation followed would strongly influence the preference.

Nevertheless, there are times in every career when a practitioner is measured against a set of criteria for competence and deemed either to have met them, or else to have fallen short. Principally, this kind of evaluation takes place during training, but there are also post-qualification requirements that define a certain standard of practice. While training establishments and accrediting organizations will vary, sometimes widely, here is a basic map for identifying these landmarks:

During training:

- criteria for entry to course;
- assessments of progress over its duration;

- requirements for award of final qualification;
- for some practitioners, meeting the requirements for accreditation by a professional organization separate from their training institute (e.g. BACP).

Post-qualification:

- continual Professional Development (CPD) and re-accreditation procedures required by accrediting bodies;
- for those in employment, meeting the performance requirements of the employer;
- maintaining the confidence of a clinical supervisor;
- less formally, being accepted by a network of other practitioners in which an individual might be embedded.

While CPD and other post-qualification procedures are important, and will be revisited in later chapters, perhaps the most definitive assessment of a practitioner's competence is when we face our final exams, or other requirements for achieving accreditation. While they may not be in the forefront of our minds in the moment-to-moment experience of working therapeutically with a client, the criteria set by training institutions and accrediting organizations are likely to influence the way each of us might define competence for ourselves, whether we are just at the beginning, or many years post-qualification. In Chapter 5, 'Becoming a practitioner', initial training is discussed in further detail.

Competence and regulation

At the time of writing, discussions are taking place in the United Kingdom between the statutory authorities and accrediting organizations about regulation. This is a topic that has been around in various forms since I began training twenty years ago – when there was anxiety about the impact of standards imposed by the European Union – and probably before that too. As the profession has grown and become more widely accepted, so the desire to regulate has gathered momentum. The debate is constantly evolving and the websites of BACP and UKCP are where details of the current situation may be accessed.

Regulation requires the setting of a minimum standard of competence that practitioners must achieve. There is continuous discussion and debate about how to do that and, indeed, whether to buy into such attempts to define and regulate. Reports from the accrediting organizations are regularly full of this kind of subject matter.

National Occupational Standards

There are some efforts being made to define a standard that every practitioner is required to meet. National Occupational Standards exist for both counselling and psychotherapy. Their purpose is to inform employers, training organizations and individuals of the precise minimum competences to which practitioners will be expected to perform. Here I use the word 'competences' to mean something similar to criteria.

The web address is www.skills forhealth.org.uk and there are links to follow to access the standards for specific professions.

UKCP has a statement of competences for psychotherapists that relate to each of its colleges. These are available from: www.psychotherapy. org.uk/ukcp_standards_and_policy_statements.html

Values underlying Statements of Competence

A tension exists between what is known as the 'medical model' and therapeutic assumptions and values. Perhaps a rough definition of the medical model would be to say that 'patients' have something wrong with them, for which an expert practitioner would produce a diagnosis and then prescribe a remedy. This is in contrast to a therapeutic model where 'clients' are seen more wholistically as a fellow human being who is currently troubled, as we all can be. Often it is assumed that the client has the answer and the role of the therapist is to facilitate the client to discover it. Some modalities, particularly CBT, and possibly some analytic approaches fit well with the medical model, others less so, and there has been a fight to have the other approaches recognized as having something valuable to offer. As an example, there is an announcement today on the UKCP website (5 January 2013) that those responsible for setting NICE Guidelines will be inclusive of the range of psychological therapies available. NICE is the acronym of the National Institute for Clinical Excellence, which is the body that defines best practice for the treatment of both physical and mental conditions in the UK.

While counsellors and psychotherapists are being absorbed into the National Health Service (NHS), doctors, nurses and other health professionals are also in a debate about how to define competence. This is what one writer on professional development for doctors has to say:

> The public expect that a qualified professional will be competent in the discharge of normal professional tasks and duties. To suggest, therefore, that professional qualifications should be designed to indicate

that aspiring professionals have completed their initial training and are now competent appears to be simply stating the obvious. However, such statements also carry other connotations. First, to make such a statement is to imply that that is not what happens in practice: not all professional qualifications certify competence; and by innuendo this 'malpractice' is common. Second, there is a hint that competence in practical matters must be preserved against the encroachments of the intellectuals. The use of the word 'competent' is not value-neutral.

(Erault, 2006: 159)

While there are tensions between the medical and therapeutic models, this extract shows there are parallels between the situation for counsellors and psychotherapists and that of traditional health professions with regard to competence. As with doctors, both the public and other professionals assume that someone is competent when they qualify as a counsellor or psychotherapist. With the range of provision available, it is likely that competence is construed differently within the various training organizations. Modalities compare themselves with one another and there is still a sense of hierarchy (Rowan, 2005). The discussion around whether there is a difference between counselling and psychotherapy is a prominent current example.

A competence paradox

While the wider environment seems to be encouraging a movement towards establishing minimum standards for competence, perhaps the reluctance to go wholeheartedly down that path arises from a particular facet of the nature of therapeutic work. Modalities would probably have different ways of describing it. Here are some examples.

In his much-respected book, *On Learning from the Patient*, analyst Patrick Casement writes:

It is all too easy to equate not-knowing with ignorance. This can lead therapists to seek refuge in an illusion that they understand. But if they can bear the strain of not-knowing they can learn that their competence as therapists includes a capacity to tolerate feeling ignorant and incompetent, and a willingness to wait (and to carry on waiting) until something generally relevant and meaningful begins to emerge. Only in this way is it possible to avoid the risk of imposing upon the patient the self-deception of premature understanding, which achieves nothing except to defend the therapist from the discomfort of knowing that he does not know.

(1992: 4)

As a Gestaltist, I would consider Casement's 'not-knowing' to be equivalent to the concept of creative indifference:

> It is clear, therefore, that there can be no particular skills or techniques associated with creative indifference. It is about the cultivation of an attitude that is at the heart of all the Gestalt skills. Being fully in the here and now, meeting with another person without preconditions, is a potentially frightening experience as well as an exciting one. We are facing the unknown and that can make us feel insecure. We can then feel a strong urge to take control by planning and predicting. As Gestalt counsellors, we should try to resist that urge and, instead, risk staying with the uncertainty.
>
> (Joyce and Sills, 2010: 40)

Carl Rogers, who originated the Person-Centred approach expressed it in this way:

> I am often aware of the fact that I do not *know* [italics in original], cognitively, where the immediate relationship is leading. It is as though both I and the client, often fearfully, let ourselves slip into the stream of becoming, a stream or process which carries us along. It is the fact that the therapist has let himself float in this stream of experience or life previously, and found it rewarding, that makes him each time less fearful of taking the plunge.
>
> (1967: 202)

It seems that, ironically, one of the fundamental competences for practitioners of some approaches is the ability to withstand feeling incompetent and not-knowing, and to be tolerant of uncertainty. For other modalities this would not be the case at all.

Competence and co-transferring

Transference and counter-transference were fundamental to the practice of psychoanalysis in the early days (Jacobs, 2004). Transference is where the client treats the therapist in the manner he or she learned by relating with a primary care-giver. Counter-transference is when the therapist behaves in that way with the client. It is also when the therapist notices her or himself responding to the way she or he is being treated by the client. This can mean that the therapist might feel a whole range of feelings that are evoked by the client: a tendency to protect or punish; wanting to minimize the client's emotional response; sexual desire. It is possible that the therapist may feel powerless or incompetent as a result of transferential forces too, either from their own early experiences, or because the responses are evoked by the client.

As the different modalities developed through the humanistic movement, more attention started to be paid to the relationship between therapist and client as people relating to one another in the present moment, and potentially less to co-transferring. When I began learning about Gestalt, it was common that any transference was 'ignored', with the emphasis being on the here and now relationship (Joyce and Sills, 2010). As time went by, its usefulness was recognized and it was talked about in the therapy-room, as well as in supervision, and was taught on training courses. Other modalities (and individual practitioners) vary in the attention they give transference and counter-transference. Awareness of the nature of the relationships we experienced in our early lives is an important contribution towards understanding whether we are being influenced by counter-transference.

A framework for assessing competence

In the previous sections I have outlined situations where competence is measured: in training and CPD contexts, and for the possibility of furthering a movement towards standardization and regulation. I have indicated where and, to some extent, why there is a broad panorama of attitudes towards defining competence, and the range of different expectations various stakeholders have of such statements.

Those of us who are already qualified have proved our competence, at least to the satisfaction of our various accrediting bodies. Those still in training will be very much working towards achieving that recognition. We have all met, or are in the process of meeting long lists of criteria. Because they are used by specific training organizations as a measure to decide whether students are ready to be accredited as qualified practitioners, they need to be specific and comprehensive. The National Occupational Standards are equally detailed. As a way of measuring moment-by-moment competence in practice, these would be too unwieldy to be held in the small (but necessary) part of our attention we reserve for assessing our own performance.

This book is concerned with understanding what work we are competent to do, taking into account our background, experience and training. It is also about the maintenance of competence at an everyday level, as we go about our work. The approach I have taken is distinct, and meant to be separate from the procedures of accreditation, CPD and regulation.

Variety is valuable, and I wanted to find a methodology that would be inclusive, and could be adapted for particular preferences because of its flexibility. I have evolved a framework that I believe is concise, practical and relevant for all.

The framework involves focusing on just three essential elements, those of:

- the practitioner
- the 'client'
- the context.

I put the word 'client' in quotation marks because, while it generally means a person involved in therapy, it could also in this context refer to supervisees, students and groups.

1   **The practitioner:** Aspects that are associated with the practitioner element involve her or his personal history, training and orientation and current life circumstances.
2   **The client:** This element concerns the nature of the 'client', the quality of the relationship and the issues that are involved.
3   **The context:** This involves the circumstances in which the therapeutic work is taking place: the organization; policies and procedures; physical space; professional frameworks; societal implications etc.

As I keep emphasizing, competence is different for each individual and depends on the unique context. Naturally, each of the three elements impacts closely on the others, but it is useful to separate them to increase understanding of them. The following chapters look more closely at each of the three elements, and are intended to help practitioners extend their awareness around the issues associated with each of them.

Each chapter explores a particular area of practice, which is condensed into a single principle. The principles offer a more-detailed structure for exploring and maintaining competence. Here are all the eight principles together:

PRINCIPLES OF THE COMPETENCE FRAMEWORK

- Cultivation of the self in relationship.
- Recognizing the impact of difference.
- Acknowledging strengths and limitations of training.
- Understanding the nature of the client and possibilities for therapeutic relationship.
- Awareness of context.
- Identifying and remedying difficulties.
- Making good use of supervision.
- Nurturing and replenishing the self.

You will see that the first three principles relate to the nature of the **practitioner**, the fourth to the **client** and the fifth to the **context**. The final three are concerned with how the practitioner can conduct their practice competently and ethically. They stand as guidelines for competent practice, and can also be used by individual practitioners, or in supervision, to shed light on aspects of therapeutic work. They offer a more detailed basis for exploration than the three elements, for situations where that is appropriate, or may be helpful.

By creating a 'Competence Framework' I am echoing the BACP Ethical Framework (BACP 2010), which has gained wide acceptance from individual practitioners and relevant organizations. I am suggesting that the Competence Framework can be used in a similar way to the Ethical Framework. Case Study 2.1 is an example of how I used the three elements of practitioner, client and context as a focus for exploring a situation that arose in my own practice.

CASE STUDY 2.1

I had been working for more than a year with a woman in her forties who was in a high-powered position in local politics. The immediate issues that had brought her to therapy were starting to be resolved and life was feeling much more satisfactory to her. We periodically talked of ending, but something would happen in her life and we would carry on working together to process it. A session occurred when she announced on arrival that this would be our last meeting. My response was to feel shocked, but somehow not surprised, and I communicated something of this to her. I reminded her that our agreement for ending had been that we would have at least one session that both of us knew ahead of time would be the last one. She said that she felt we had been talking about finishing for weeks. I agreed that we had, but explained how important it was to attend to the process of ending by setting a specific date. I also disclosed that I felt uneasy that there was something not quite complete about the work. She was adamant that it was time to go, and we said a final goodbye at the end of the session. I was left feeling that an old pattern of ending had been re-enacted and that I had not been skilful enough to draw her attention to it in such a way that she was willing (or able) to give it consideration. Overall, while it seemed that my client was pleased – and she was fulsome in her acknowledgement and thanks – I felt I could have done better. Naturally, I took it to supervision and, after much thought and deliberation, believe I would do better when a similar situation arises again. I had misinterpreted why she talked about ending yet did not definitively state that she wished to bring our sessions to a close. I think I overestimated her ability to be clear about her own needs in relation to mine. I understand that, at this point in my practice, it is the ending that can be the problematical stage, and I am particularly vigilant around them now.

The part of the Framework that I considered relevant here was to do with who (and how) I am as a practitioner. The client was an appropriate one for me, and our ways of relating to one another were generally adequate, so that part of the framework was not where the difficulty lay. There was no particular issue to do with the context either. Having identified the relevant element of the framework, I was able with the help of my supervisor to bring my tendency to find difficulty with endings into awareness, so as to have that increased understanding to support myself with in the future. The following chapters will explore in detail how each of the three elements can be used to explore competence.

Chapter summary

Discussions of the occasions when competence is measured were highlighted, and possible mediating factors in the recognition of competence were defined. A Competency Framework that is adaptable for all orientations, and any stage of training was introduced. The Framework has three elements around which practitioners can define what competence is for themselves and measure how competent they are being in moment-by-moment work with clients.

The elements are:

- Practitioner
- Client
- Context.

The three elements are the basis for the eight principles of the competence framework.

ACTIVITIES

Individual reflection

2.1   When, specifically, do the occasions on which your competence is assessed occur?

In supervision

2.2   Are there occasions when the competence of either supervisor or supervisee, or both is evaluated? By whom, and for what purpose?

Group activity

2.3   How would you assess your competence as a group? Depending on the size of the group, this exercise may need to be done in stages, with sub-groups having discussions and then feeding back.

PERSONAL REFLECTION

Every January, I'm required to submit a return to my accrediting organization, the Gestalt Psychotherapy Training Institute (GPTI). The form asks me to state the number of supervision hours I have under-taken and give details of the continuing professional development (CPD) activities in which I have participated. It also asks about any reading, writing and committee work I may have done, as well as any particular personal development or spiritual practices I have adopted.

At five-yearly intervals I go through a re-accreditation process. This year I'm about to do that for the third time. It involves forming a group with four to five others who are re-accrediting in the same year and meeting together, usually for a day. Each individual produces a report to describe the current circumstances of their practice and, during the meeting, talks it through with the other participants. They then question the individual in a way that is meant to be both sup-portive and challenging. A consensus is then arrived at as to whether it is appropriate for the person to be re-accredited. Sometimes there is a request for a modification in the way the individual practices. A report of the whole event is prepared and forwarded to the GPTI office, together with the reports of individuals.

While these structures are in place, and I find benefit from com-plying with them, I feel I have to establish my competence in every session I have with a client or supervisee. This is particularly so because I work mainly in private practice, so people have to pay me out of their own pockets. If they don't find our meetings helpful, they will quickly stop coming. Naturally, I don't get everything right. If a strong enough working alliance (Clarkson, 1995) exists between us, then I can be forgiven. Indeed, working through difficulties can be a powerful reparative experience. Therapy can be painful, bor-ing, frustrating and irksome. Remarkably, people will continue with it, particularly if there is an explicit understanding this can be so.

The constant discipline of being present, attentive, sensitive, quick-thinking, tolerant of powerful feeling states, professional and as wise as I can possibly manage to be, takes a lot of energy. I am wondering now how much effort to be competent actually is required and whether other practitioners might think I give too much or try too hard.

Chapter 3

The development of self

Chapter outline

Exploration of the Competence Framework begins with identification of the major factors that contribute towards the individuality of a practitioner. The first of them, which concerns early life experience, is examined in more depth here. A brief overview of psychoanalytic theory from Freud to the end of the twentieth century, focusing particularly on theories of child development, is offered. These ideas, and the ways they have been modified and enhanced through time, provide outlines for thinking about engaging with clients therapeutically. They also offer potential structures for exploration of a practitioner's own background and early experience, bringing into awareness factors that may strongly influence client work, allowing potentialities and limitations for competence to be better understood.

Practitioner individuality

The primary element of the Competence Framework is that of the Practitioner. Our individuality emerges from the coming together of all the various facets that make us into who we are, both as a person and as a practitioner. Each of us is different, and our strength lies in that uniqueness. Inevitably, so also does our weakness, which is why it is important to develop a deep understanding of how we are formed as a practitioner. Such an insight allows us to identify when we are being as competent as it is possible for us to be, and when we are falling short of our individual standard.

The practitioner is the focus for the Competence Framework because her or his competence is what is being examined. The client (or supervisee, or student) will change; the context of the work will change, but the practitioner remains the constant factor. That is not to say that the practitioner will not change. Indeed, one of the underlying premises of this book is that practitioners want to grow and develop themselves as both people and professionals. Working therapeutically with others seems to evoke expansion.

Major contributing factors in the development of a practitioner are:

- early life experience (including issues of difference and diversity);
- initial training;
- impact of current life experience;
- ongoing professional development;
- impact of therapeutic work.

Early life experience includes the circumstances in the family of origin that contribute so greatly to the way a person develops. It spans the traumas that may have been experienced: abuse; bullying; serious illness and accidents to self or someone close. Relevant too are the individual's sense of self and the nature of the relationships that were developed with other people. There may also be issues around food and addictive substances or practices. This segment is concerned with the choices that have been made: the recognition of achievement; the loss of people or opportunities; guilt or regret for what has taken place. It is also associated with the significant issues around culture, ethnicity, gender, sexuality, ability, and other aspects of diversity, which are explored in a separate chapter.

Initial training makes a significant contribution to the way a practitioner is formed. This facet explores: the motivation to do therapeutic work; reasons for choosing a particular course, and modality; the experiences a student is exposed to while training; the relationships that were formed with tutors, fellow-students and others in the organization; how competence was conceptualized and measured; the attitudes and behaviours that were implicitly and explicitly valued. This is discussed in Chapter 5.

Impact of current life experience explores how the practitioner's life situation is affecting their practice. Bereavement, illness, stress, money issues, worries about family members and many other factors may influence therapeutic work.

Ongoing professional development includes discussion of further training in specialist areas like supervision, couples work, therapy with children and adolescents etc. CPD and re-accreditation procedures are also relevant, as is the effect of progression in a particular workplace, or in the profession generally.

Impact of therapeutic work is concerned with the effect that working with people that are in great distress, even severely traumatized has over time.

Each of these factors is explored in more detail in Chapter 6.

Structures for exploration

Training in counselling and psychotherapy involves being introduced to theories about human beings. A variety of concepts of child-development are commonly taught on training courses, and each modality has its own ideas of what good, or not so good functioning might look like in adults. Most of us, then, will have some theories with which we can understand how individuals come to be how they are, and some ways of facilitating beneficial change. Indeed, these form the theoretical base from which we work with our clients. The concepts that underpin the different modalities often influence the context and style of their training, as well as the content. Students on some courses may be expected to learn about theories by means of recollecting their own early experiences, and giving and receiving feedback from other students and tutors about the way they are currently perceived. Others may experience a more academic approach, with theories being understood at an intellectual level. Personal therapy may or may not be a requirement of a course and so opportunities students have for gaining insight from it vary. Whatever our experience of training, and the modality we have chosen, we are likely to feel that we have been along a path of personal development. We may or may not co-relate that to our ability to work effectively with clients.

Bager-Charlson (2012) describes her research into therapists' reasons for choosing to enter the profession. Seventy per cent of respondents gave childhood or adult crisis as their motivating factor. That many of us are wounded healers implies that we may have missed out on some early childhood experience, and are seeking to make up the deficit. This is one reason that I believe practitioners who want to work in a reparative, relational way with their clients need to undertake personal therapy. Alice Miller (1995: 4) claims that 'The repression of injuries endured during childhood is the root cause of psychic disorders and criminality. The price of repression and denial in childhood, however necessary to the child, is the symptoms of the adult.' With this statement she makes it clear that the 'repression', or non-acknowledgement of childhood hurts is what causes difficulty; bringing them into awareness can allow for integration and their becoming eventually less troublesome. While she establishes a clear link between childhood experience and adult functioning, she acknowledges by implication that the child has to make adaptations in order to survive the circumstances in which they find themselves, and that the adaptations are often a brave attempt to deal with a difficult situation in the best possible way. Later in the same passage (1995: 4), Miller insists that 'therapists who ignore their own childhood history can disturb, hamper and delay' the process of gaining insight in the client.

Of course, it is possible to work effectively in some approaches without having done personal work. Rowan (2005) defines what he calls Instrumental, Relational and Transpersonal perspectives. Examples of modalities that are included in the Instrumental perspective are solution-focused, brief and cognitive and/or behavioural approaches. Person-centred, bodywork therapies and Gestalt are examples from the Relational category. The Transpersonal group includes Jungian, Core-process and Psychosynthesis practitioners. Difference is good, and each of the approaches has advantages they can offer to clients, meeting the range of needs people have from therapy. It is probably helpful for each of us to have a sense of where we are in our own practice, because it will help us to know when we might be moving out of our areas of competence. Our position may change over time. When I first became familiar with Rowan's model I was firmly in the Relational category. Now I notice myself moving towards the Transpersonal.

Family of origin

In this chapter we are considering the family of origin and early life, so it seems appropriate to begin with psychoanalytic/psychodynamic approaches, because of their understanding of our very early experiences and the impact they may have on us as adults. These theories began to be formed in the earliest days of psychotherapy as we know it currently. By tracing the work of some of the major contributors to the field, they illustrate the development of the analytic strand of the profession over time.

Guntrip (1968: 361) reports Winnicott's belief that 'it is the mother–infant couple that can teach us the basic principles on which we base our therapeutic work'. So the reparative work undertaken in therapy is likely to follow and mirror a child's early upbringing, hence the interest analysts have in understanding the experience of the infant, and what 'good-enough' mothering might entail.

Melanie Klein considered that,

> to be immature is to be acutely at the mercy of impulsive fluctuations which can swamp the mind with anxieties, rages and passions.

Children are therefore emotionally dependent on adults for the regulation of their states, and not, as previously believed, dependent in a purely material and educational sense.

(Likierman, 2001: 2)

When clients who have had insufficient containment of emotion in their early lives look to us as therapists for a reparative experience, we are unlikely to be able to provide it unless we have had enough of it for ourselves either, if we are fortunate, in our family of origin, or else by means of our training and personal therapy.

Theories of child development

For those who want to begin or extend an exploration of early experience there are many models. Several of them may already be familiar because they are commonly introduced on training courses across all modalities. Some of them will feel more congenial to individuals than others. What follows is a brief overview of certain of the theories that are generally accepted as significant landmarks in the development of the profession, and are well-known. It is not meant to be exhaustive, but offered in the spirit of being a 'taster': for some a reminder of the breadth of thinking available, for others a brief introduction to theories that might evoke interest and be a signpost towards further learning and insight.

It is reasonable to begin with Freud's (1905) model of psychosexual development because it is probably the earliest for psychotherapy, as we know it currently. Its oral, anal and phallic stages are accomplished with some sort of resolution of the Oedipal dilemma by around age 6, when a child moves into the latency period, before adult sexual functioning begins with the onset of puberty. To a certain extent, the stages follow the baby's immediate physical experience: the acceptance of nourishment; the rejection of that which is toxic, or not wanted; the recognition of difference.

Barden (2006: 41) acknowledges that 'Freud's account of the development of gender identity through the Oedipus complex seems very outdated these days. It is best approached with an appreciation of his own starting point and context – as the originator of psychoanalysis, theorising from his own small sample of patients within Viennese culture.' Whatever our view of his assumptions about gender roles, symbolized by the possession or lack of a penis, it is likely that we can acknowledge the significance of gender in our sense of self. Freud's theory also highlights the significance of the entry of an other (father in Freud's world, but not always in ours) into the mother and baby dyad, and gives significance to the sense of similarity or difference with same or opposite sex parents or carers.

CASE STUDY 3.1

I worked with Graham, a man in his sixties at the time we were meeting. He lived with his mother, who had a disability and was also frail because of her age, and he took care of her. He was an only child and his father was long dead. Graham had been married in the past, but had not been in relationship for a while, and was looking for prospective partners on internet dating sites. After our fifth session, he rang to say that his mother was ill so he would not be able to make our next scheduled meeting, and was not sure when he would be available in the future because that would depend on his mother's condition. He said he would ring when she was better. I never heard from him again. My assumption was that it was easier for Graham to be involved in the difficult, but familiar and predictable relationship with his mother than it was to forge something new and different in therapy with me.

When I was training in Gestalt, the developmental model came from Fritz Perls' book *Ego, Hunger and Aggression,* which was originally published in 1947 (Perls, 1992). Perls was one of the challengers of Freud's approach and the cover of the book proclaims it to be 'A Revision of Freud's Theory and Method'. Perls was more directly concerned with eating than with sex and his theory focuses on the progress a baby makes from sucking, to biting, to chewing. Following the stages of a child's ability to engage with food, the model is extended to include the way he or she can engage with the world in general. At first, a baby can connect only with what the care-giver has to offer, and in a limited way: sucking and being sick. When front teeth appear, it is possible to cope with a greater range of what is available, and be more selective because we can spit out anything that is unacceptable for us. Sometimes this stage is associated with becoming aware in adulthood of any introjects we may have taken on: beliefs or assumptions that we have not fully 'chewed' and that may be causing us difficulty, for example the belief that we must always put others' needs before our own. Therapy or training can offer a chance to re-consider, and either reject the introjects, or assimilate them fully. The appearance of back teeth allows us to grind even tough food, or ideas, so as to be able to obtain nourishment from them. In my training group a lot of emphasis was placed on the ability to spit out. We were encouraged to place a piece of dry cracker into our mouths, and then make a decision about whether to chew it up and swallow it, or to spit it out. Spitting out is not conventional social behavior, so we had to overcome that sense of prohibition. Having done so, we could explore our own readiness to accept or reject what was on offer, which many of us found insightful. Perls' model would probably not be the only one taught these days, as Gestaltists have responded to the wider field, and the requirement for understanding child development in a fuller way. Yet it does highlight the interdependence of self and 'other' that is fundamental to gestalt thinking. We constantly take from the environment what is necessary to meet our needs, whether it is food, oxygen, love, learning, beauty or any other requirement. Other people are, of course, a significant provider of these necessities, and we give and take from one another in accordance with our relationship styles.

Melanie Klein's theory of development involved a progression from what she called the 'paranoid-schizoid' position to the 'depressive' one. At the beginning of life the infant experiences 'a paranoid-schizoid position, characterized by splitting mechanisms and primitive persecutory anxiety' (Likierman, 2001: 115). The child cannot conceptualize a mother who sometimes meets her or his needs and at other times fails to do so, and so creates a split between good mother and bad mother. With sufficient integration comes the depressive position: 'good' and 'bad' can both be contained within one person, whether it is the child or the carer: 'The more the infant perceives of reality, the more whole her understanding, the more she is obliged to face a distressing world which has loss and pain in it' (Likierman, 200: 90). The child is able to accept that the same mother can sometimes meet his or her needs, and sometimes not. While the depressive position is seen as a developmental step forward, it is accepted that even as adults we move between one and the other. Ogden (1992, in Teicholz, 2001) describes the process in this way:

> It is important that one not pathologize the negating, de-integrative, decentering pressures associated with the paranoid-schizoid component of the Ps<—>D dialectic [the back and forth movement between the Paranoid-Schizoid and the Depressive Positions] ... In the absence of the de-integrative pressure of the paranoid-schizoid pole ... the integration associated with the depressive position would reach closure, stagnation and 'arrogance' (Bion, 1967). The negation of closure

… represented by the paranoid-schizoid pole of the dialectic has the effect of destabilizing that which would otherwise become static. In this way, the negating de-integrative effects of the paranoid-schizoid position continually generate the potential for new psychological possibilities (i.e., the possibility for psychic change) [p. 616].

(Teicholz, 2001: 117)

So we need to revisit the bewilderment and intensity of the paranoid-schizoid position as a precursor to deep change. I remember my own therapist reassuring me when I was feeling particularly disorientated by telling me confusion was a good thing (M. Parlett, personal communication).

By the 1980s, Stern was observing real children, rather than making theoretical assumptions from how a person is as an adult. He claimed that 'The notion of the mouth as especially endowed as an erotegenic zone, in the strict sense that Freud and later Erikson meant, has not borne up in general observation or in attempts to operationalize the concept of erotogenic zones as developmental realities' (1985: 235). While Freud's (and Perls') models are not validated by actual observation, they still may have some usefulness as metaphors for experience. With Stern, the focus moves from the physical body, and internal psychological processes to the 'in-between'. Stern emphasizes the significance of relationship for the development of a baby's sense of self. 'The sense of a core self is a perspective that rests upon the working of many interpersonal capacities' (p. 26–7). The concept of 'self' is important for Stern and his work describes how a baby's sense of self evolves from birth. He remarks, 'Is not the infant's initial experience thoroughly social, as the British object relations school has taught us?' (p. 101). In doing so, he acknowledges the significance of the object relations practitioners for understanding how early relationships are formed.

Jacobs describes object relations theory in this way:

Much modern psychoanalytic theory is called 'object relations theory', a term which partly means 'personal relations', but also includes the partial relationships people have with 'objects' as well, and which thinks not just in terms of relationships between people, but also within each person, where 'internalised' representations of external relationships also play an important part in a person's make up.

(2004: 4)

Donald Winnicott is probably one of the best known practitioners of this approach. While earlier theories focused on the experience of the individual child, Winnicott emphasizes the indivisibility of child and mother. His term 'transitional object' (1958: 229–42) is used to describe a blanket or toy that represents mother for a baby to help him or her deal with separation. It is also used for the book or other item that a client may borrow to tide over a long or difficult gap from therapy. In a similar way, carrying an internal representation of mother (or therapist) may be seen as helpful. Many clients tell me that, after we have been seeing each other for a while, they begin to deal with difficult situations by imagining what I would say, or even imagining hearing my voice, and so avail themselves of my support even when I am absent.

Bowlby's theories of Attachment are also validated by Stern's research: 'Some levels of attachment, such as the behavior patterns that change to maintain attachment at different ages, can be seen readily as sequential phases of development, while others, such as the quality of the mother–infant relationship, are life-span issues' (Stern, 1985: 25). Bowlby's attachment styles and concept of a secure base are such useful ways of thinking in a therapeutic context, particularly one that is long term. Many potential clients arrive in my office describing how they cannot fully commit to a relationship, usually with a partner, and asking if I can help. Thanks to Bowlby's description of the ambivalent attachment style, I am able say to the prospective client that I probably could help, if they felt able to commit to coming to therapy, even though they may at times be ferociously unwilling to do so. I explain how a similar dynamic to that with the partner might occur with me. If that were to happen, it would give the person an opportunity to work through those feelings in a, hopefully safe, manageable environment, with my support. I have also met many clients who show characteristics of Bowlby's avoidant attachment style, people who come to understand that they long ago gave up any hope of having their needs met by, initially primary care-givers, and then by anyone. The ways that people find to adjust to this lack are many, and discovering and mourning them can often be a significant part of the therapy. Clients with secure attachment style may still arrive seeking therapy. Perhaps some trauma, loss, illness or long-term challenging situation will bring them to seek support. People who have been exposed as children to significant neglect are said to have a chaotic attachment style, which may mean that they experience significant difficulty in even making it to sessions, and could possibly require the additional support of an agency to benefit as fully as possible from therapeutic work.

Stern does take issue with Winnicott and others' assumptions that 'the infant cannot adequately differentiate self from other'. Because of this he claims that, '[t]he infant can be with an other such that the two join their activities to make something happen that could not happen without the commingling of behaviors from each'. This last extract returns me to the nature of the therapeutic meeting. The emphasis shifts slightly from the concept of a therapist who gives and a client who receives, to a situation in which both parties co-create an encounter that is inventive, and also unique to those particular individuals in that precise moment.

Another important contributor working around the middle of the twentieth century was Heinz Kohut. He called his approach self psychology and believed that, in order to achieve an adequate sense of self, a baby needed to experience an environment that offered four important functions: the soothing and containing of powerful emotions; a mirroring by and with another person; twinship, which meant the sense of belonging among a group of similar beings, and the idealization of a parent figure, so that the child could identify with her or him and be strengthened as a result (Teicholz, 2001: 86). An adult entering analysis would need to experience a similar environment in order to make good the deficits in her or his sense of self. Since Freud, analysts had sought to present a blank screen to their analysands, the better to invite the transference that could then be brought to the analysand's awareness by means of interpretations. In sharp contrast, Kohut (1984) emphasized the importance of warmth and empathy from the analyst.

Kohut's work was taken up by other practitioners and, as a result of 'the multiple and partially overlapping contributions of Ogden, Stern and Stolorow et al.' (Teicholz, 2001: 183) the term 'subjectivity' started to be used as an alternative to 'self'. 'Intersubjectivity' was used as a way of describing the relationship with an other. Analysts began to understand the limitations, and even impossibility of the blank screen, and to use their own subjectivity (or difference) within the therapeutic relationship. This meant that, potentially, the internal processes of the analyst could become as much the focus as those of the analysand: 'Analytic exploration of both intentional and unwitting self-revelation is in the forefront of current psychoanalytic discourse' (Teicholz, 2001: 143).

This implies that a classically trained analyst might use self-disclosure in a similar way to a Person-centred counsellor, although probably with a different theoretical rationale. The strands of the analytic and humanistic approaches seem to join together around the significance of the therapeutic relationship.

Implications for practice

Over time the emphasis developed from a one-person psychology to a psychology of relationship. Being trained in Gestalt, I naturally look at these theories from that perspective. They seem similar to the Gestalt notion of an organism (a human being with a body) being embedded within an environment (which includes other people, and also other beings and the world in general). An individual is in a complex relationship with 'other' and each has a profound impact. The 'co-created field' (Joyce and Sills, 2010) influences both parties in the therapeutic encounter too, with each potentially being changed in the process.

A human being, whether called an 'organism', a 'self' or a 'subjectivity' is affected by contact with an other, and has an effect in return. The sense of being an individual is formed in relationship. Our work is often concerned with the outcome of this process having gone awry in some way. Winnicott's (1965) theory of 'false self' is one way of understanding how a child might have to make so many compromises to survive that the 'real self' is ignored and forgotten. Some of these deficits can be made good in therapy. The intersubjective, or co-created nature of the encounter may result in some beneficial change for either of the parties involved. For a therapist, competence involves purposeful cultivation of the self in order to develop authenticity and robustness. How is that achieved? Through relationship, naturally. Whether as children with our families of origin, or as adults with our therapists, trainers and supervisors, we can grow into the person we really are. The ability to engage with clients from that place certainly makes us more competent, and is likely to make us more effective too.

The version of the story of psychoanalysis I have offered brings us to the first principle for the Practitioner element of the Competence Framework:

Cultivation of the self by and for relationship

Conclusion

At this point, the two themes of this book, competence and self-care, coincide. The self is what we bring to the therapeutic encounter, and also the means for engaging therapeutically with a client. The development of a refined sense of self generally is and, I believe, needs to be an outcome of initial training. The self is further developed by ongoing training and development, and professional and life experience generally. It is likely to become depleted and tarnished by the challenges and vicissitudes of engaging with an other. When that happens, ways of restoring and replenishing robustness need to be sought.

Chapter summary

Significant factors influencing the development of an individual practitioner were defined as being:

- early life experience (including issues of difference and diversity);
- initial training;
- ongoing professional development;
- impact of current life experience;
- impact of therapeutic work.

An overview of the development of psychoanalytic theory identified the importance of relationship for creation of the self, and of the self for the creation of relationship. Theories of child development illustrated both how early relationship defines a practitioner's sense of self, and how relationship can heal through the practice of counselling and psychotherapy. The first principle for the Practitioner Individuality element of the Competence Framework was defined as:

Cultivation of the self by and for relationship

ACTIVITIES

Individual reflection

3.1 Journal around your family of origin, perhaps using one of the theories as a focus. Arrive at a point where you can define one thing from your early experience that is helpful for you in your work as a therapist, and one that makes things more difficult for you.

In supervision

3.2 Explore how your relationship with your supervisor may, and may not have some similarity to your relationship with a close family member in the past.

(Continued)

(Continued)

Group activity

3.3 Draw a house in the manner often used by children, perhaps with a winding path to the front door and a chimney with smoke swirling. Pair up with another person and tell them a story about the people who live in that house. Talk about how that was for you, and then change over and listen to the other person's story. In groups of six to eight (depending on size of group and available time) tell the story belonging to the person in your pair. It doesn't have to be completely accurate, feel free to embellish it, adding details that occur to you in the moment as you tell it. Listen to your own story told back to you and notice how any changes that may have been made affect you.

PERSONAL REFLECTION

I had both studied and taught most of the concepts I decided to include in this chapter. Re-visiting them in sequence in the way that I did allowed me to see patterns in the way ideas were developed. Certain passages in books took on a new significance for me. Kohut's (1984: 8) definition of psychosis, 'central hollowness, but a well-developed peripheral layer of defensive structures', was a perfect description of someone I was meeting with at the time. As I pondered it more fully, I realized it could also have been a description of my mother. I could see clearly why her protestations of love, sincerely meant as they no doubt were, had left me with such uncertainty about my ability to let myself be loved; something I saw played out in my life more than I actually felt. If there is too little sense of self, then the ability to engage meaningfully with an other is impaired. The discovery was painful, but now I know, there is the possibility for change, both in my personal life and with my clients.

Chapter 4

The diverse self

Chapter outline

The impact of gender, ethnicity, culture and other aspects of diversity on an individual is examined. Ways to gain awareness of how people can be different are highlighted, and the relevance this has for practitioners as individuals is explored. There is a discussion of the composition of the profession, and how the cultural backgrounds of the majority of practitioners may affect issues of diversity, particularly the accessibility of therapy for members of minority groups. The second principle of the Competence Framework is introduced.

Gender, ethnicity, sexuality, disability and other issues of diversity

To further understanding of the Practitioner Element of the Competence Framework, I explore how the sense we have of our selves in relation to difference influences us as practitioners, and discuss what might help to increase competence for working sensitively around matters associated with difference and diversity. I offer my personal experience of the ways that people can be different from one another, focusing on categories that seem to be significant in our society. I invite readers to make a similar exploration of their own relationship to diversity, by means of a number of suggested activities. Working therapeutically with people significantly different from ourselves, and those with whom there are potentially other issues related to diversity, is explored in Chapter 7.

Aspects of diversity

> Engaging with difference and diversity at a deep level is challeng-
> ing and leaves no assumptions undisturbed, no values and beliefs
> unchallenged. It can be profoundly disturbing.
>
> (Wheeler, 2006: 5)

Even deciding which categories to include as areas for exploration feels
problematical. Here are the ones I've chosen. Naturally they reflect
my own experience, although they parallel those identified by others
(Wheeler, 2006).

ACTIVITIES

Activity 4.1a

Notice how you feel when you look at this list. Maybe there is an
emotion you can name. Perhaps there is a body sensation you can
become aware of... Write anything you notice in your journal.

- gender;
- ethnicity and culture;
- sexual orientation;
- class;
- religion and spirituality;
- physical and mental ability or disability;
- age.

Activity 4.1b

What do you think about this list? Are there any categories you don't
think should be included? Are there any categories that should be
there but are missing? Write your own list of categories for diversity
in your journal.

For the purposes of this discussion, I am using the word 'difference'
to describe how one person may be unlike another. For example, I
like to practise yoga. Other people may prefer pilates, football, golf,
or not to take any exercise at all. 'Diversity' describes how certain of

our characteristics may cause us to include ourselves, or be included by others, in pre-identified groups; or else, equally, that we do not feel included in such pre-identified groups. For example, I am white. Others are black, or brown, or mixed race. Immediately a differential of power or privilege comes into play.

At this point, I have noticed how, in my first, supposedly simplistic example, about physical activity, I have taken it for granted that everyone is able to make a choice about taking exercise. Clearly that is not the case. I take many of the privileges I have for granted, so much so, that I don't even notice them a lot of the time (Ryde, 2009).

Counselling and psychotherapy have been developed in Europe and, more recently, North America (Lago, 2006: 82). Readers of the previous chapter, where I briefly discuss key theorists in the history of psychoanalysis, may have noticed that they are, in the vast majority men, and members of the middle-classes. That some of them, including Freud, were Jewish, is interesting to note and may, to some extent account for the movement of ideas from eastern Europe to western Europe and the United States, as a result of the political situation in the early twentieth century. Other major therapeutic approaches show a similar pattern of predominance by men. The profession has inevitably been influenced by their point of view. The categories I have identified as being relevant for the discussion of diversity are those that deviate from a white, male, middle-class norm.

Gender

Ironically, while many of the influential thinkers, writers and leaders in the profession are men, most of the practitioners in everyday roles are women. When I meet with colleagues, in whatever context, women usually outnumber men. In the training groups I work with, men are usually in the minority. Male counsellors and psychotherapists are generally self-aware, sensitive, emotionally articulate and warm. In some ways, the profession is dealing with a dynamic of gender relationships that is different from that in the wider society, in other ways it is not. While amongst therapists, there can be sufficient insight to predict and understand feelings that might arise from being part of a minority group, attending to men's feelings of isolation or disempowerment from being in the minority in a professional context, can be problematic. 'Resentful feelings surface when the focus is on male worldviews, female therapists sometimes experiencing men as occupying "centre-stage" with women in the wings' (Aitken and Coupe, 2006: 75).

The same writers observe:

> The feminist movement and equal opportunity legislation have contributed to redressing the power balance between men and women. For years there has been a focus on the growth and development of women, so much so that being asked to consider the social and psychological role of men is unexpected and unfamiliar for some women.
>
> (Aitken and Coupe, 2006: 75)

Even in the benign professional context of counselling and psychotherapy, women and men working together have to negotiate a complicated power differential. It may often be ignored, but if it is acknowledged and explored, then it can be brought more fully into awareness for all those involved. As practitioners, whether male or female, we can help our clients to address issues around difference, but only if our own assumptions, attitudes, biases and preferences have been explored. Part of the exploration is likely to be around how the genders are different. Perhaps inevitably, women's experience is described in the way in which it differs from that of men:

> Joining ... understanding of women's psychological development with theories of human development which turn out to be theories about men, I have arrived at the following working theory: that the relational crisis which men typically experience in early childhood occurs for women in adolescence, that this relational crisis in boys and girls involves a disconnection from women which is essential to the perpetuation of patriarchal societies.
>
> (Gilligan, 1993: xxiii)

This extract not only challenges the relevance of Freud's Oedipal dilemma for women, but also describes how the psychological processes of both women and men may contribute to the maintenance of a culture that disadvantages women. The question of whether psychological theory and practice serves to maintain the status quo has relevance for other categories of diversity too. Is that inevitable? Is it that people are who we are and professionals are only describing what is there to be observed?

Winnicott (1986) tells us that individual identity is created and embellished through the process of fantasy by the internalisation of part objects, aspects of people, who are in turn influenced by systems, societies and cultures. Social and political movements affect society and social structures in turn affect the nature of the self.

(Wheeler, 2006: 11)

This extract challenges that assumption. It is possible that the wider environment in which a child's family of origin was placed influenced the family, and in turn influenced the development of self in the child. The implication of this is that the self emerges in relation with intimate other, but also embedded in a wider context, which is powerfully influential. This theme is revisited and developed in Chapter 8.

ACTIVITIES

Individual reflection

4.2   In your family of origin, how did being the gender you are affect the way you were treated? How were others of the same gender treated? And others of a different gender? Journal for 10 minutes.

In supervision

4.3   Explore how each of you is different from the other. This could be an obvious difference like gender or race, or a subtle one, like religion or class. Are there some differences that are too difficult to talk about?

Group activity

4.4   Divide into groups along gender lines. Distil three statements that define 'What is it like to be a woman/man/other in this group?' If all group members are the same gender, discuss what that might mean for the group.

Ethnicity and culture

I am Welsh, which means that I have access to all the privileges that being white and western offers. Being Welsh is different from being English. While it is a gross generalization, my experience is that English people have more confidence, affluence and sense of entitlement than Welsh. Maybe this is a consequence of the history of the two nations. Although I consider myself Welsh, my family came over from Ireland about three generations ago. I still remember visiting my grandmother Bridget (my father's mother) in the area of Cardiff called Newtown. Situated near the port, and neighbouring the notorious Tiger Bay, it was a traditional Irish enclave. Bridget spoke with an Irish accent, as did many of her neighbours. I grew up during the time when Irish nationalists were planting bombs on the British mainland, and I remember how sensitive my parents were about being Irish Catholics in some contexts then. My maternal grandmother, Esther, was the daughter of a European Jew.

As an immigrant, I am unable to speak Welsh and feel I am denied access to the rich culture of music, art and poetry that flourishes in the various Eisteddfodau (gatherings to compete in a range of arts-related categories) that take place. The history of South Wales is that of exploitation of coal and iron. The Englishman, William Crawshay was a major figure in the industrialization of the region. In many ways, it feels like Wales was colonized too. Whether it is appropriate or not, this perception leaves me feeling less guilt, and more envy than some others who may look and seem similar (Ryde, 2009). Of course, this could be a self-deception.

Kapadia (2008) offers a way of understanding differences in cultures that is helpful for increasing awareness around each of our own cultural backgrounds. The model is also useful for therapeutic work with clients from different cultures. She differentiates between *individualistic* and *collectivistic* societies. Western culture is more individualistic, with the emphasis being on the cultivation of each separate person: non-western cultures tend to prioritize the interests of the family and wider community. Failure to understand these different perspectives in a therapy context may lead to either of these values systems being pathologized, a particular danger for a practitioner in the prevailing western culture, where it is possible that a collectivistic world view may be seen as less adapted to the current society. Having an awareness of cultural differences may help inappropriate pressure to conform to an individualistic (or collectivist in some situations) paradigm to be avoided.

Naturally, it is important not to assume that someone from a particular ethnic group or cultural background will follow the values system more associated with that culture, nor to imagine that a person will fit neatly at one end of that continuum: reality is always more nuanced. Here are some signposts to the nature of the difference between the collective and individualistic cultures.

Continuum of current individualistic society	Continuum of collective society
Birth – privacy of nuclear family, naming parental responsibility. Adolescence – leaving home.	Birth – baby is a public celebration. Naming is a family function. Adolescence – stay at home, respect elders, girls restricted.
Love marriage (Eros) – youth is revered.	Arranged marriage (Agape) – love marriage. Couple live in extended family.
Elderly live alone or in care homes.	Wisdom is revered. Responsibility to care for elders.
Private mourning.	Collective grieving, rituals.

(M. Kapadia, Personal Communication, 2009)

While the majority of counsellors and psychotherapists still seem to be white, practitioners from minority ethnic groups are speaking about how cultural expectations influence the therapeutic relationship and framework. This is enlightening and enriching for all practitioners, as assumptions that are believed to be true of everyone, but in fact that are only true about some people, are brought into awareness.

Understanding what it means for us as individuals to belong to our own race and culture helps us to maintain competence in our work with others, whose experience will be different, however alike they may seem to be.

ACTIVITIES

Individual reflection

4.5 What is the balance between collectivistic and individualistic values for the culture in which you were brought up? Journal for 10 minutes.

In supervision

4.6 Explore with your supervisor the similarities and differences between the cultures to which each (or all) of you belong. How does that affect the way you work together?

(Continued)

(Continued)

Group activity

4.7   Divide into two smaller groups. Group A takes a collectivist paradigm and group B an individualist. Discuss in sub-groups your expectations of the whole group from your given standpoint and list on a flip chart. Share in full group and discuss.

Sexual orientation

I am bisexual, which means that I have had sexual relationships with both men and women. I notice how hard it is to write that in a context where the information might permanently enter the public domain. Despite civil partnership having been available for many years, and a bill to allow gay marriage currently being discussed in the UK parliament, I still feel exposed by the acknowledgement. Maybe my expectations belong to the past, when being gay could not be talked about; it had to be kept hidden except in exceptional circumstances and, of course, among other gay people. Perhaps I have a natural reticence about discussing sex, which is private: heterosexual people do not generally have to think about whether they need to disclose their sexual preferences, in order to be fully known.

Being bisexual is not the same as being gay. Davies and Neal (1996) observe that:

> Few people exhibit an exclusive sexual orientation. Yet the myth of dichotomous sexualities continues to be pushed by both the heterosexual and homosexual communities. This is distinctly unhelpful since it creates a false division into what is acceptable and is extremely inaccurate.
>
> (1996: 3)

Jung had a 'vision of a psyche based on polarities, in which transformation is found in 'the *union of opposites through the middle path*' (Jung, 1917:203 (emphasis in original), quoted in Barden, 2006: 44). He believed that:

> men and women carried within them, biologically and psychologically, traits of the 'other' gender. These traits have an active

existence in the psyche and, if not acknowledged, are projected onto actual men and women, usually in an idealised or devalued form. For Jung, male and female formed two parts of a whole, and the expectation of the other is present from the start.

(Barden, 2006: 44)

Jung's concept of the 'union of opposites' may offer a way of resolving Davies and Neal's 'myth of dichotomous sexualities'. If, as Jung implies, individuation involves the integration of polarities, then we may be well served by recognizing the aspects of ourselves that are masculine and feminine and those that are heterosexual and homosexual: to embrace the opposites rather than try to deny one of them. This way of thinking has come to be known as non-dual. Ryde (2009: 115) states that '[t]he most fundamental way of understanding non-dualism is to see reality as the mystics from all religions view the world – as interconnected and undivided'. She goes on to explain how non-dualistic thinking can help overcome potentially irreconcilable differences when working with clients. I will return to this in Chapter 7.

While being able to integrate opposites within ourselves, and in our client work is a great advantage, we live in a world that is also (maybe predominantly) dualistic in its attitude and behaviour. People do define themselves as either heterosexual or homosexual. Homosexual men and women tend to be called by different names. At the moment, homosexual women are commonly known as lesbians and homosexual men often refer to themselves as gay men. However, they are bound together in a category called 'LGBT' (Lesbian, Gay, Bisexual and Transgender). In my experience, same-sex relationships are different from opposite-sex ones. Couples may often socialize with other same-sex couples and the opposite sex can become irrelevant and even alien. The stereotype is of the plain and practical lesbian and the glamorous, stylish gay man. Nevertheless, sharing a sexual orientation can make alliances attractive. While they tend to be bound up in the LGBT category, transgender people can, of course, have a same-sex, or an opposite-sex orientation.

Sexual preference can be invisible. Generally, it is possible to identify a person's gender and race (although we cannot assume we always get it right). It is possible to hide sexual preference, on some occasions, or on all occasions. For some gay people, their appearance gives them away and others make immediate assumptions about them (although those are not always right either). Despite the liberalizing of western society, prejudice is still to be found. 'Coming out' can be a significant thing.

ACTIVITIES

Individual reflection

4.8   Where do you see yourself on the heterosexual/homosexual continuum? How do you feel about this? Journal for 10 minutes. Afterwards, do something that feels nourishing for your self. (Look at Self-care section, Chapter 11, Part II, for suggestions, if necessary.)

In supervision

4.9   How much do each (or all) of you need to know about your respective sexual orientations in order to work together effectively? Focus your discussion on consequences for bringing client work with people from different sexual orientations.

Group activity

4.10   Journal individually for 10 minutes, imagining the experience of someone with a different sexual orientation from yours. What might it be like to be that person? Share first in groups of three to four, if numbers are large, otherwise discuss in full group. Is there anything that might need to be shared?

Class

Class can affect the way we see the world; the expectations we have, the demands we can or cannot make. Class may also influence the amount of income we have at our disposal. Becoming a counsellor or psychotherapist is expensive, especially for those involved in a long psychotherapy training. A requirement for personal therapy substantially increases the cost, and may exclude people with lower incomes. Inclusivity is one of the arguments in favour of courses that do not require personal therapy.

In British society, people from what is called the middle class are likely to have more money, better paid jobs and a higher quality education than people from what is called the working class. 'There is ... a great deal of evidence suggesting social class remains the single most powerful determinant of life-chances (Child Poverty Action Group, 2004; Collins, 1994; Kearney, 2003; Social Dimensions of Health Institute, 2004)' (in Isaac, 2006: 157). Some blurring of boundaries between the classes exists now, with people being able to move more easily from working to middle-class. Greater access to education is a possible contributing factor to this situation. I consider myself to be working class. I was brought up in an overcrowded terraced house and money was tight. To others, I probably seem middle-class because of the way I look and speak, and because I got myself an education. Despite this, the difference I notice between what I expect from life and what properly middle-class people expect is stark. Entitlement was one of the significant issues I dealt with in my personal therapy.

I was able to fund my training because of a redundancy package from a previous employer. Most of the other students in my course were middle-class. Some of them defined themselves as upper-class (and had that lifestyle). Most of the colleagues I work with currently are middle-class. The clients I see in my private practice need to be able to afford to pay my fees, so the majority of them are professionals. There are exceptions, and I have met with people with lower incomes who are willing to invest in themselves by seeking therapy. I notice that many of my most financially-stretched clients seem to be counselling and psychotherapy trainees!

Some practitioners, students or clients can be sensitive about their privilege. The validity of accusations that 'talking therapies' were the province of the relatively well off has been easily recognized. Widening availability has become an issue of concern in the profession, in terms of both prospective clients and potential students hoping to enter the profession. Over recent years, counsellors have been available in some GP practices, as well as in specialist agencies in the voluntary sector. Concerns about employee welfare, particularly around the levels of stress experienced in some occupations have led to employee assistance provision that includes counselling, being made available to their staff by a variety of companies. All these initiatives have widened the range of people who can benefit from counselling whether they are those who might not otherwise have been able to afford it, or those who were previously unfamiliar with it. Longer-term therapy is likely to be unavailable except to those who are willing to finance it for themselves, other than in exceptional circumstances.

The class with which we as practitioners associate ourselves, and those of the clients we meet in the various contexts in which we work, can be as much an issue of diversity as gender, ethnicity and sexuality, although it is not so often discussed (Isaac, 2006). It could be seen as a matter of power, with some groups being more likely than others to expect to have their voices heard.

ACTIVITIES

Individual reflection

4.11 Journal for 10 minutes, exploring how your class and access to money have influenced your development. Is there anything you were unable to do because you could not afford it? How has this affected you?

In supervision

4.12 Who pays for the supervision? What does that mean for the work?

Group activity

4.13 Split into two sub-groups. One group discusses the profession from a working-class point of view, the other from a middle-class. Chart up some expectations you have of the way you expect your career to progress. Share in full group.

Religion and spirituality

Society has become more secular over recent decades, although increased diversity has widened the range of religions that people may be in regular contact with and are likely to follow. I call myself a pantheist now, meaning that I believe in all religious systems although I was brought up Catholic.

Religion can be divisive. I have particular experience of the antagonism between Protestants and Catholics in the twentieth century in the UK. Fortunately, things have improved greatly since then, although there are different focuses for religious difference now, both here and in other parts of the world.

Some people would say they were spiritual, rather than religious. In this context spiritual is likely to mean that a person is sensitive to the numinous, but not associated with any particular group. Ross (2006: 175) asserts that 'Counsellors and psychotherapists cannot remain neutral about religion and spirituality as to do so is to fail the client by not attending to their whole psyche.' This implies that everyone has a spiritual element to their psyche so, as practitioners we may be concerned with exploring and developing our own as a way of increasing our competence with clients.

ACTIVITIES

Individual reflection

4.14   What was the relationship to religion and spirituality in your family of origin? How does that affect you currently? Journal for 10 minutes.

In supervision

4.15   Is there a transpersonal (or spiritual) element to the way you work together? Discuss.

Group activity

4.16   How many people identify themselves as religious? Or spiritual? Or with no connection at all to the concepts? Divide into sub-groups along those lines and discuss your experience. Afterwards share anything relevant in full group.

Physical and mental ability or disability

When I work with groups of students I often ask if anyone considers they have a disability. I can be surprised by the result: people with obvious physical constraints may not include themselves while others, who look able-bodied may talk about their invisible disabilities, like deafness or dyslexia (Shakespeare, 2002 in White 2011). There can be an invisible absence: people whose conditions mean they are unable to access the building in which the training is being held, and those who are excluded by less direct causes, lack of money because of being unable to work full-time, or at all, for example.

I do not consider myself to have a disability, although I do have experience of needing to use a walking stick for several months. When I turned up with my stick to somewhere I wasn't known, to make a presentation or run a training people seemed wary. White (2011: 13) asserts that '[t]he discomfort that we seem to experience in the presence of impairment is so universal … it might be a hardwired human trait.' I really felt that discomfort!

Mental health is a particularly sensitive area for therapists, because it is where we see ourselves being effective, but also where, in some situations, the limits to our effectiveness can become apparent. We may have had experience of mental health issues ourselves, or with another member of the family and, for some of us, this may be one of the main reasons for our entering the profession. My mother suffered a number of what were known in those days as 'nervous breakdowns', a term which seems to cover a lot of possibilities but nothing particularly specific. She spent long periods in hospital when I was a child and I have vivid memories of going to visit her there every Sunday afternoon. It seemed a long time between one Sunday afternoon and the next. I never told anyone at school about it; I think I instinctively felt a stigma. Anyway, I wasn't the kind of child who talked about feelings. If any of the teachers noticed I was behaving differently, then they did not mention it. I think my early experiences have given me an easy tolerance of the manifestations of mental ill-health. When I did the twenty-day psychiatric placement I was required by my training organization to undertake, I went to a local acute unit and found it rather a familiar experience.

'(P)eople fear and avoid disabled and disfigured people' (Segal, 2006: 94). Reeve reminds us that:

> Counsellors are subject to the same negative images and stereotypes of disabled people as the rest of society. The attitudes and prejudices of counsellors towards disabled people can adversely affect the nature of the client–counsellor relationship when the client is a disabled person – there is sometimes oppression within the counselling room. Whilst counsellors are aware of the need to challenge their racist and sexist attitudes … many counsellors are aware of their disablist attitudes which remain unrecognised and unchallenged.
>
> (2000: 669)

This is a reminder and a challenge for all of us.

ACTIVITIES

Individual reflection

4.17 What was your experience of either physical or mental illness or disability in your family of origin? How does this
influence you as a practitioner? Journal for 10 minutes.

In supervision

4.18 Discuss how you approach physical and mental illness and
disability in your supervisory relationship.

Group activity

4.19 Who considers themselves to have a chronic illness or disability, either physical or psychological? Maybe they would
be willing to talk about how it affects them in the group, and
in everyday life.

Age

In western society we are coming to terms with an ageing population. As
well as actually living for longer, many of us are able to remain vigorous
and in good health as we grow older. My grandmother died at 63, after an
illness that lasted three weeks, once it became acute, and had looked like
an old woman for several years before her death. Nowadays, I see people
in their sixties and seventies doing vigorous workouts in the gym and,
for many of them, looking like they are in their early fifties. Conversely,
when we become frail, we stay alive for a lot longer. My mother died at
age 80, having suffered ten years of declining health, mobility and (to me)
quality of life.

'Old' is difficult to define and probably depends on the age of the person making the decision. I notice that I am starting to be treated as 'old'
by some people in their teens and early twenties. At its worst, I am spoken
to as if I'm not a real person any more. The communication is by means
of simple language, delivered in a highly-enunciated manner, and without
eye contact. I notice that I can treat people who to me seem 'old' as if they
are somehow different from me. I probably speak more loudly and choose
topics that are quite mundane. I try to be conscious of it, and stop.

I have had very few clients I considered 'old'. The culture in which people were brought up was different, and counselling was less familiar (Wellington, 2006). Freud (1905a) did not believe older people could benefit from psychotherapy. The generation of people that are now beginning to become 'old', sometimes known as the 'baby-boomers', were involved with the personal growth movement led by Carl Rogers, Fritz Perls, Virginia Satir, and others. Therapy is seen as a way of life (and a career) for many of us. That being the case, it is likely attitudes and expectations will change, and older people will expect access to therapy.

The English Longitudinal Study of Ageing (ELSA; the full findings from the ELSA study can be found at www.ifs.org.uk/ELSA) identified that, '[i]n general, older people with better psychological wellbeing are protected from physical disability and coronary heart disease and remain fitter and more active into later life' (Jackson, 2012: 6). Counselling and psychotherapy could make a significant contribution to maintaining that wellbeing. After all, if the alternative is death, most of us will hope to be old. Maybe we could campaign to have services in place to serve our own interests at a later stage, as well as those of clients now.

ACTIVITIES

Individual reflection

4.20 What does being your current age mean for you? Journal for 10 minutes.

In supervision

4.21 Is there an age disparity between you? How does the way you answer that question impact on your work together?

Group activity

4.22 Make a sculpt of the group by forming a line according to age, starting with the oldest at one end and the youngest at the other. Notice how it feels to be where you are. Allow an opportunity for individuals to step out of their place and look at the whole line. Participants may also want to try a different place in the group and have a feel for how it is unlike their original position. Process in pairs initially, then in full group.

Implications for practice

Counsellors and psychotherapists are not generally a very diverse group. Some of us may feel that neither we nor our clients fully reflect the nature of our society. Perhaps as a profession that specializes in relationship and communication, we are in a very good place to enter into a dialogue with each other about these matters. Doing so might support us in our work with clients, and also help us to integrate ourselves more fully in the knowledge of our own issues of diversity.

The first principle of the Competence Framework was defined in the previous chapter as:

Cultivation of the self by and for relationship

A second principle to join it, distilled from this exploration of diversity is:

Recognizing the impact of difference

Conclusion

Exploring the categories of diversity can be a way of bringing to awareness aspects of our selves that we may have previously taken for granted. It can be challenging and even painful to do so, but I believe it is ultimately for our own benefit, for that of our clients, and for the wider society in which we live. We cannot be separate from our environment and may choose to act towards it in a way that promotes our own values system within it.

In Chapter 7, I look at diversity from the point of view of working with clients from different cultures.

Chapter summary

Categories that are of particular relevance to issues of diversity were defined as:

- gender;
- ethnicity and culture;
- sexual orientation;
- class;
- religion and spirituality;

- physical and mental ability or disability;
- age.

Following a personal exploration of these issues, the second principle of the Competence Framework was introduced:

Recognizing the impact of difference

The chapter contains many suggestions for activities the reader can undertake to explore their own relationship to issues of diversity.

PERSONAL REFLECTION

Writing this chapter involved covering a lot of ground, both as far as the different theories are concerned and in the exploration of my own diversity. For the theories, I re-encountered some writers who feel like old friends. Some of them actually are teachers and colleagues. The personal exploration is more of a risk in a book like this one but, if I am encouraging readers to be honest with themselves, I can hardly do less myself. There is a potential for shame to be evoked by acknowledging difference. It is possible to offend others' deeply held convictions whilst expressing our own. I wanted to be able to undertake these tasks adequately and honestly, and take care of myself while I did so.

Chapter 5

Becoming a practitioner

Chapter outline

The initial training chosen by a practitioner will have a significant influence on the competence of that individual. Trainings differ in duration, subject matter and style of facilitation. Understanding what a training has made a graduate competent to be and do, is important when overall competence is being measured. The experience of a small number of graduates is described in their own words.

Introduction

Exploration of the Practitioner Element of the Competence Framework continues with a discussion of the training required in order to practise as a counsellor or psychotherapist. The choice of an initial training is an important one. The theoretical orientation, content and style of the training will influence the kind of practitioner a student will become; also, because of the nature of counselling and psychotherapy training, it is likely to influence the kind of person a student will become.

When I tried to find out exactly how many counselling or psychotherapy courses were available in the UK, I was unable to compile a definitive list. Many trainings are accredited by BACP and UKCP, and can be identified through those organizations, but others are accredited by the training organization that offers them, usually a university or college of Further Education.

One significant distinction seems to be between trainings that describe themselves as counselling courses, and those that are described as psychotherapy courses. Generally 'psychotherapy' courses are longer than 'counselling' courses. They have different content and requirements from one another. 'Counselling' courses are more likely to be accredited by BACP than 'Psychotherapy' courses, which are accredited by UKCP (which also accredits Psychotherapeutic Counsellors). With no protection of titles, graduates of any course (or no course at all) could potentially call themselves counsellors or psychotherapists, or an alternative.

BACP have taken the initiative of accrediting training courses that meet a certain standard. Being accredited by BACP means that a course meets rigorous criteria and that students graduating from them have a more direct route to being accredited as practitioners by BACP. Here are the criteria that training organizations are required to have their students be able to meet if they wish to have their courses awarded the benchmark of BACP accreditation.

B1.3 The course must show how the course applicants are assessed for the following attributes or the potential for developing them:

   i. Self-awareness, maturity and stability
   ii. Ability to make use of and reflect upon life experience
  iii. Capacity to cope with the emotional demands of the course
  iv. Ability to cope with the intellectual and academic requirement
   v. Ability to form a helping relationship
  vi. Ability to be self critical and use both positive and negative feedback
  vii. Awareness of the nature of prejudice and oppression
 viii. Awareness of issues of difference and equality
  ix. Ability to recognise the need for personal and professional support
   x. Competence in, or the aptitude to develop generic professional skills, including: literacy, numeracy, information technology, administrative skills, self-management skills, communication and interpersonal skills

www.bacp.co.uk/admin/structure/files/repos/416_course_
accreditation_scheme_pdf (retrieved 19 December 2012)

The situation is different in UKCP, with training providers joining together in colleges, and being subject to their own accreditation and quality control procedures. Examples of some of these appear later in the chapter.

Choice of initial training

Potential students are likely to be influenced in their choice of course by a personal attraction to the package a particular provider offers. Frequently, choice is limited by the amount of money a potential student has available. Both counselling and psychotherapy courses are expensive. Longer courses are more expensive, as an initial outlay, than shorter ones: practitioners may choose to supplement a shorter training by undertaking additional training after graduation. Shorter courses mean that, potentially, a student can begin to earn money sooner. Requirements for personal therapy have a huge impact on cost. When it is mandatory, it can add many thousands of pounds to the overall cost of training. Travel costs may also restrict the choice to a provider that is geographically close.

Money, time and travel arrangements can be such enormous influences that potential students may lose sight of other important factors like: 'Will this training get me where I want to be, both professionally and personally?' It feels difficult for potential students to find the answer to that question, as they make comparisons between the possibilities available to them.

Some potential students are strongly influenced towards organizations where they feel some sort of 'fit'. If there are trainers from minority groups highly visible in an organization, then they are likely to attract larger populations of students from that group. For example, black potential students may prefer to work with black trainers; gay students with gay trainers; students with disabilities with trainers with a disability.

CASE STUDY 5.1

Oonagh was expecting her first baby. She decided to take the opportunity to make a career change and train as a counsellor. Her plan was to return to her demanding job in retail on a part-time basis after her maternity leave, and combine care for her child with undertaking a counselling training. She wanted to minimize

(Continued)

(Continued)

the amount of travelling involved, so applied to two local training organizations. The first accepted her unreservedly and discussed with her how she might make special arrangements for the baby to accompany her on the residential element of the training. The other organization explained that Oonagh might find the content of their course, and the nature of their approach to training very challenging while she was in the relatively early days of becoming a mother. They also asked her to consider her motivation for undertaking a challenging course while there would be many demands placed on her as a carer. Oonagh decided to undertake her training with the first organization.

Reflection points

How might you account for the different responses from the two training organizations?
What might the benefits and drawbacks for Oonagh be, resulting from her choice of organization?

ACTIVITIES

Individual reflection

5.1 Write for 10 minutes without stopping, about the reasons you chose the training course you did.

In supervision

5.2 Discuss with your supervisor the extent to which an issue that may concern you about a particular client is connected with the theoretical orientation of your initial training. (My difficulty with client endings, described in Chapter 2, has direct links with Gestalt, where there is a lot of emphasis on avoiding 'unfinished business' (Joyce and Sills, 2010).)

Group activity

5.3   Discuss what attracted you to your particular training (in sub-groups of four to five if the group is a larger one). (This activity can be done with a group undertaking initial training together, or one with a mixture of training backgrounds.)

Practitioners' experience of becoming qualified

The criteria students are required to achieve in order to be considered to have met the requirements of the course are a measure of what competence might look like for graduates of that training. But can they be generalized, so that an ordinary member of the public would be able to understand what to expect from the profession as a whole, and from individuals within it? I began to gather sets of criteria from a range of different sources. Some of the sets of criteria are extremely lengthy. This is to be expected because training organizations and individual students need to know specifically the standards that are required to be reached.

Training Institutes define criteria that their students must meet in order to graduate. On the face of it, there are many similarities. Most involve:

- knowledge of theory;
- proof of ability to do the work ethically and effectively over time, and in a manner that fits with the underpinning theory;
- evidence of self-development;
- academic skills, sometimes emphasizing research.

Having found so much information, I felt that I needed to ground it in some way, so as to be able to make sense of it. From my own experience I knew it was likely that the ways in which students demonstrate that they have met the criteria would differ, depending upon the ethos of the organization and reflecting the values of the approach being taught.

For example, I happen at the moment to be a staff member at the Bath Centre for Psychotherapy and Counselling (BCPC). In BCPC, where the approach is Humanistic Integrative, but the psychodynamic is a significant element of the training, it is common for student groups to be considered as though they are families, with tutors taking a parental role. In my own Gestalt training students were expected to be grown up and self-reliant, relating with tutors in an adult-to-adult way. This fits with the theoretical framework set in place by the founders (Perls, Hefferline and Goodman, 1951).

Where counselling and psychotherapy courses are embedded within a wider training organization, like a university or college of further education (FE) I have noticed that they are influenced by the ethos and atmosphere they experience within the environments in which they are set. In my experience there can be a more generally academic and less specifically therapeutic 'feel', and may as a consequence be particular emphasis placed on the more academic aspects of the course, rather than the personal development and relational ones – and this is not always the case.

Research

Rather than make comparisons of sets of criteria for accreditation, I decided to try and gain a deeper understanding of different practitioners' actual experience of their initial training. In order to achieve this, I chose to do some research. The original idea involved a plan to ask graduates from a range of different orientations to look at the original assessment criteria set by their training organization and to describe how they felt they had been assessed to have met them. This was a valid way of undertaking research because from looking closely at the experience of a few individuals, it is possible to learn as much as from looking at the experience of a greater number in less depth: 'The farther afield we fly from the firm ground of immediate experience, the more diffuse and solipsistic our language becomes. And the more illusion we generate' (Roberts, 1999: 37).

I began the research process by doing the exercise myself. My accrediting organization is the Gestalt Psychotherapy Training Institute (GPTI), which is a member of the Humanistic/Integrative (HIPS) College of the United Kingdom Council for Psychotherapy. The qualification permits me to use the description, 'Gestalt Psychotherapist'. Thanks to GPTI for permission to use the following extract.

GPTI LEARNING OUTCOMES

1 The student will be expected to:

Discuss in detail the principles of Gestalt psychology and field theory, and demonstrate their application in clinical practice.

Show awareness of other major psychotherapeutic approaches, and their relationship to Gestalt Psychotherapy.

2 The student will be expected to:

Demonstrate understanding of existentialist thinking as it applies to the practice of Gestalt psychotherapy.
Understand and demonstrate competence in the use of phenomenological method. Understand Beisser's 'Paradoxical theory of change', and demonstrate application of this theory in clinical practice.

3 The student will be expected to discuss the principles of the dialogic approach and demonstrate this approach in a variety of settings, e.g. clinical practice, training settings, supervision.
4 The student will be expected to:

Discuss in detail the theory of contact and withdrawal processes in the context of field theory and dialogue.
Demonstrate the ability to maintain contact with self and others in a variety of situations.

5 The student will be expected to discuss and critically evaluate:

The Gestalt theory of self, including id, ego and personality functions.
Gestalt and compatible theories of human development.

6 The student will be expected to demonstrate knowledge and competence in the:

Initial and ongoing assessment of the client and the clinical work in relation to:

(Continued)

(Continued)

the therapist's limits of competence;
the form of therapy offered;
the prevailing field conditions, including setting;
the form of therapy offered;
the limitations of the Gestalt approach.
Development of the therapeutic alliance.
Identification of the processes of transference and counter transference, and ways of working with them in the therapeutic relationship.
Maintenance of the psychotherapeutic relationship, e.g. dealing with issues that may confront the psychotherapist, including conflicts, over identification and boundary issues.
Ending of the psychotherapeutic relationship.

7 The student will be expected to map the process, direction and progress of the psychotherapy:

Through recognition and identification of an overall shape or form to the clinical work, as well as patterns and themes emerging both spontaneously and over time.
Identification of the foci for change, the nature of the change process and the patterns of resistance to change and their meaning.
Understanding of cultural, racial, age, disability, sexual orientation, class and gender dynamics within the psychotherapeutic relationship.
Understanding of the variety of psychotherapy forms available, i.e. individual, group, couple, family, brief and long-term psychotherapy.
Awareness of how therapeutic choices are made in the context of the chosen mode of psychotherapy, e.g. brief term, group, individual.

8 The student will be expected to demonstrate theoretical and clinical competence in working with body process including:

An awareness of the client's and their own sensory, physical, physiological and affective experience.

Awareness of sexuality, and how this may impact on the therapeutic relationship.

Knowledge and skill in the use of touch in the psychotherapy relationship.

9 The student will be expected to demonstrate understanding, skill and creativity in the practice of experiment within the context of the psychotherapeutic relationship.

10 The student will be expected to demonstrate understanding of the:

Gestalt concepts of creative adjustment and contact styles and how awareness of the concepts may enhance client understanding.

Gestalt forms of diagnosis and psychopathology, e.g. fixed gestalts, decreased ego functioning.

Other diagnostic categories related to Gestalt diagnoses, e.g. DSM-IV.

Implications of working with specific client groups on clinical practice.

11 The student will be expected to show awareness of Gestalt psychotherapy as a lived discipline and relate his/her own growth to professional Gestalt psychotherapy practice.

12 The student will be expected to:

Demonstrate their integration of professional and ethical principles into their clinical practice.

Use reflection, discussion and ongoing supervision to assess and report on their own and others' work with clients.

Autonomously use resources for learning.

(Continued)

(Continued)

> Prepare for and make effective use of supervision.
> Engage confidently, respectfully and co-operatively in professional communication with others.
> Show awareness of boundary issues, including confidentiality, in specific settings. Show a basic awareness of legal issues relating to psychotherapy.

13 The student will be expected to understand Gestalt approaches to group process and how these relate to other approaches within groups and organizations and the student should have some knowledge of group facilitation skills.

14 The student will be expected to demonstrate awareness of research findings appropriate to Gestalt psychotherapy.

www.gpti.org.uk (retrieved 21 December 2012)

After I had studied the list of criteria for qualification I wrote this:

MY INITIAL TRAINING

I'm writing this because I'm trying to identify a focus for what I want practitioners to explore about how competence was measured in their initial training. Now I'm feeling excited because I have the sense of coming close to what I'm looking for. The lists define the criteria but what I want from contributors is a sense of how these criteria were measured, both overtly and covertly.

Now I feel sad because I realize I felt very much alone going for my exam. I felt like I had to say I wanted to go through the process, rather than ask if people thought I was ready. So much the rugged self-reliance I had to have in my family. I'm feeling desperately sad now. Thinking about my mask of the Duffer in challenging situations. And it is a mask. Just as much as the highly competent, coping masks others have.

So the chief measurement of competence in the gestalt community at the time was an ability to withstand highly-stressful, unsupported situations. The admired attributes seemed to be self-directedness and 'authenticity' (I put it in inverted commas because in some ways it was an aggressive assertion of self).

Some of what I wrote originally I have decided not to disclose. It was too personal and too painful. In a sense, I was surprised by the strength of my emotional response to reflecting on my experience of graduating, even after so long a time (15 years). As a consequence of writing the above, I was able to define the questions I wanted my research participants to consider:

QUESTIONS FOR RESEARCH PARTICIPANTS

Please consider the following questions and write your responses. They may evoke some feelings, so I suggest you write an uncensored first draft. You can make decisions later about what to exclude in both your sharing with me, and what is eventually published.

What attributes were most prized in your training? (overtly or covertly) Who decided?
Which were seen as most undesirable? (overtly or covertly) Who decided?
Who decided when you were 'ready'?
Who was involved in the qualification procedures? (People you had previously known, or 'outsiders'?)
What difference did it make?
How did you feel about it all?
What are you left with now?

My first volunteer research participant was a colleague of mine at BCPC. BCPC offers two routes to qualification: a Diploma or MA in Psychotherapy and a Diploma in Counselling. The MA is accredited by Middlesex University and graduates are affiliated to the HIPS College of UKCP. They would use the description 'Integrative Psychotherapist'. Here are the criteria for successful completion:

BCPC DIPLOMA/MA IN PSYCHOTHERAPY

Programme outcomes

A Knowledge and understanding

On completion of this programme the successful student will have knowledge and understanding of:

Humanistic and integrative concepts.
Psychotherapeutic theories including the humanistic, object relations, self psychology & intersubjective schools.
The therapist/client relationship.
Issues of mental health and illness and the role of psychotherapy.
Research methods within psychotherapy.

B Cognitive (thinking) skills

On completion of this programme the successful student will be able to:

Critically apply theoretical perspectives to clinical issues.
Constructively criticise concepts.
Critically analyse research and the literature.
Demonstrate originality in thought and argument construction.
Have a critical understanding of human development and self-formation.

C Practical skills

On completion of the programme the successful student will have attained:

Reflective criticism of their client work, including their part in the therapeutic relationship.

Formulation and presentation of structured arguments.

Self-direction and creativity in their learning and practice.

Working integratively and ethically.

Debating issues of theory and integration.

Management of the therapeutic process from the beginning to the end of a therapeutic intervention over time (minimum two years).

D Post-graduate skills

On completion of this programme the successful student will be able to:

Manage a practice of several clients in a responsible and ethical manner over time.

Critically analyse and reconstruct /deconstruct arguments and theory.

Manage teamwork and learn from peers.

Have personal initiative and responsibility for own learning.

Plan their work.

Conduct research and make an original contribution to theory and practice discussions and feedback, researching and writing the dissertation and case study and the ongoing supervision of their practice.

www.bcpc.org.uk/files/images/MA%20Psychotherapy%20 Student%20Programme%20Handbook.pdf (retrieved 21 December 2012)

The Counselling Diploma is accredited by BACP. Graduates use the title 'Integrative Counsellor'. It is possible, and not uncommon, for students to achieve the counselling qualification and return at a later stage to undertake the psychotherapy training. The criteria are different from those of the MA, and are to be found at: www.bcpc.org.uk/files/docs/Counselling%20Yr%202%20and%203%20HANDBOOK%20 Workbook%202012-13%20FINAL.pdf

My research participant happens to be a graduate of both programmes. This is what the participant wrote:

RESPONSE TO QUESTIONS

I trained at Bath Centre for Psychotherapy and Counselling (BCPC), having spent two years prior to this on a Person Centred Counselling training at Bridgewater College. I began my training at BCPC on the Diploma in Humanistic and Integrative Counselling. Having completed this, I decided to continue directly onto the Psychotherapy training, which I completed three years ago gaining an MA in Humanistic and Integrative Psychotherapy. I refer to myself as a Humanistic and Integrative Counsellor and Psychotherapist.

My sense is that the attributes most prized in my training were authenticity, integration and inclusion. There was an emphasis on exploring one's own psychobiography as a self reflective process and in order to more fully understand theorists in the context of their own 'story'. This involved a deep valuing of personal therapy as a corner stone of growth and learning. Vulnerability and 'not knowing' were encouraged, as was the ability to 'be with' another in their suffering. Equally important was the fostering of an atmosphere of creativity and playfulness in which the possibilities of therapy could emerge. Much emphasis was placed on the co-created nature of therapeutic work. Trainees were encouraged to find their own style of working by being true to their feelings and trusting the unfolding processes unique to each therapeutic encounter. Thus experiential learning and heuristic research were valued above academic prowess or empirical findings. Supervision was of pivotal importance in our training and seen as fundamental to the process of holding and processing trainees' work.

What was seen as undesirable was a concretizing or reifying of theory. Therapeutic ideas were not to be 'swallowed whole', but chewed over and critiqued in the context of opposing or contrasting theories and also the trainees' experience. However, this was not an excuse for 'woolly' or unsubstantiated written work – clear and informed critical analysis was a key part of the assessment procedure. Whilst many different ways of working were explored – for instance short-term solution focused methods in the Counselling Training, and bodywork or mindfulness practices in the Psychotherapy Training – the training as a whole steered away from skills based techniques, putting the emphasis on the person of the Counsellor/Therapist. What was also discouraged was any attempt to 'fast track' the training by cutting corners or speeding through tasks/assignments/experiential process. Getting in touch with feelings and deepening process was seen as a vital, and sometimes time consuming, element of the course that could not be rushed.

Who decided what was prized, or undesirable, in the training? Tutors and Trainers both created and reflected the ethos of the organisation. This was modelled by the Course Directors and overall Head of Training, all of whom also taught on the training. BCPC employed a mix of staff who had qualified in other training organizations, as well as ex-students who had trained within BCPC, to ensure ongoing diversity and avoid 'stagnation' of ideas and practices. Students' input was also valued and encouraged through facilitation of student-led learning in the form of seminars and workshops, both within the training days, and also during CPD events. The BCPC Association allowed students to voice their opinions of the organization and its practices and to run some BCPC events. A Central Committee of the BCPC Association was historically run by students. Various other committees essential to the running of BCPC were predominantly made up of volunteer BCPC graduates (i.e. Re-accreditation, Standards and Ethics, Training). There was also a Graduate body within the umbrella of the BCPCA which was dedicated to the ongoing needs and interests of the BCPC community post qualification. As a registered charity, BCPC was run under the auspices of a Board of Trustees, which included BCPC graduates and members of the wider community who combined business acumen with psychological minded-ness.

(Continued)

(Continued)

Who decided when you were 'ready' to qualify? Again, this would ostensibly be the Tutors and Supervisors' decision, but it is important to underline the student's part in the process; self and peer assessment was a key part of the process, combined with joint feedback co-created by tutor/supervisor and student. Thus student's 'readiness' was determined within a holding container of the training, whilst also encouraging an inner 'authority' in the student to be able to feel into his or her own sense of readiness. If I could use one word to sum up 'readiness' in the context of BCPC training, it would be 'integration'.

Who was involved in the qualification procedure? In order to qualify a student needed to submit a written dissertation, case study and self assessment. They were also required to show proof of ongoing weekly (at least) therapy with an accredited practitioner approved by BCPC for the duration of their training. Also, a supervisor's report containing amongst other things confirmation of the required number of client hours completed by the student. Trainees chose two internal (BCPC staff known to them but not their current Tutor or Supervisor) and one external examiner to read their written work and mark it. In some cases the external examiner was known to the student, but not always. In the case of the Psychotherapy MA, the dissertation would also be sent away to be marked by assessors from the University of Middlesex, who were unknown to students. The whole submission 'package' would then be assessed at a special Board Meeting involving the student's Tutor and other BCPC members.

It is an interesting question to ask what difference did it make to have external assessors involved in the qualification process. My own experience is of two quite different processes of submission. When I submitted for my Counselling Diploma I was barely aware of external assessment or 'criteria' – although there were some, they were either from the BCPC 'fold', or chosen by BCPC as 'aligned' to the ethos of the training. My memory is of an exciting, but not too arduous process of submission. When I read my Counselling dissertation now, I can almost feel the enjoyment I felt when writing it ... it is very creative, vibrant, almost care-free.

My Psychotherapy MA submission had to be sent to external university examiners, which was an entirely different process. Whilst my initial ideas about my research topic seemed to flow easily, in the writing up I found myself floundering. Feedback from my Tutors was positive, but towards the end of the process, and nearing the submission date, they expressed concern as to the overall feel of the writing. It was deemed 'eclectic' as opposed to 'integrative'. With a week to go before submission, and with the help of the Tutor's rigorous critiquing and feedback, I re-wrote large sections of the dissertation with an eye always on the assessment criteria. I remember it as one of the hardest weeks of my life! I felt caged, reined in, shackled – the discipline required to write within the constraints of strict rules of criteria was huge, and arduous for me.

However, reading back my dissertation now, I can feel all the hours of struggle, the writing and re-writing, the chewing over and discarding, the picking out of the most salient points. There are few extraneous words. The process I went through to 'give birth' to the dissertation is almost tangible to me on the page, and is testament to the process of integration – I felt visceral at times – that I experienced in the writing.

I suppose I could draw parallels with my own process of submission and the differences between Counselling and Psychotherapy: my training in Counselling was shorter in duration and didn't 'touch' me at such a depth as my Psychotherapy training. However, there was certainly also a natural progression in terms of my own personal journey – going forward into my Psychotherapy training I had the benefit of all the personal therapy, supervision and experience of agency work and private practice gleaned from my Counselling training. This, paradoxically perhaps, led me down into a deeper, often more painful and ambivalent place. Less care-free and light. More dark, shadowy and complex.

(Continued)

(Continued)

Looking back at both processes now, and with the benefit of hind-sight, I am left with a sense that both are valuable and interesting, and very appropriate to where I was on my own journey at the time. And with that in mind, I would not wish them to be any different.

Two particular points stood out for me when I read this. I noticed how my participant's experience of completing the psychotherapy course had an element of pain in it too. I was beginning to wonder if this would be a theme that would emerge – as if it were necessary to visit a place of darkness in order to complete some rite of passage. I also noticed how the participant differentiated between the counselling and psychotherapy trainings, finding psychotherapy 'more dark, shadowy and complex'. I wondered if this also would emerge as a theme.

In an attempt to find more participants for the research, I asked around in the network of practitioners I know, looking for people with an analytic or transpersonal background, to widen the perspective. It was hard to find people to respond. Of course, I had no idea of the reasons that made people reluctant. One obvious factor would be the time it would take out of busy lives. I speculated that I was asking people to be vulnerable and, despite assurances of anonymity, they might want to avoid the possibility of being exposed in some way. I also considered that if, as I was beginning to believe, the process of graduating had some pain associated with it, then that would be a reason to avoid reflecting on it.

Eventually, I made an appeal for participants at a BACP networking event and five people agreed that I could email the questions to them. Two people responded.

The first responder had undergone a transpersonal training. The participant wrote:

I trained at Synthesis, a training organisation based in Bristol that operated until 2003 offering Psychosynthesis training. I qualified over three and a half years with a Diploma in Psychosynthesis Therapy & Counselling. It permits use of

*'counsellor', 'therapist', 'psychosynthesis guide', 'psycho-
therapist', 'transpersonal therapist' – in a context outside of
protected or regulated titles. Attributes prized in my training
initially were around emotional embodiment and willingness/
readiness for experiential process individually and in group.
I think covertly there was a bias towards engagement with
'exotic' practices and life experiences. I was the youngest on
my training by 10yrs so this factored in also. I needed to prove
myself, not academically as that was initially less valued (and
part of my own comfort zone) – but in terms of the will, resilience, commitment, steadfast ability to stay with it (especially
challenging as I had a job at the time – most of my peers were
only studying the course and were seen as more committed to
begin with). Later values shifted into imagination, creativity,
therapeutic awareness and presence – this coincided with the
'green light' to work with real clients – a massive deepening
of the course. Also, by that point over half the initial group
had dropped out. Decisions as to what seemed valued came
from the top down initially, from the course director. This was
reified in group process, then later challenged, deconstructed,
owned, rejected, remade ... Ultimately I think I decided what
I valued and explored that with others, but it was an arduous evolution. Undesirable qualities, at least for me initially,
seemed to be around the rational mind, the intellect, the capacity to analyse, critique, write well. Everything I knew of being
a student got inverted to begin with and instead of deep prob-
ing subtle debates about the relative merits of Kohut or Wilber
I had to find a way to integrate people spending whole PD
sessions howling out cathartic goddess rage or arguing about
whether we could open a window or not if someone objected.
I was confounded, startled even, but ultimately it moved on,
people left, space opened up and a variety of teaching inputs
from a range of other tutors and guest speakers rescued me by
valuing my contributions and recognising that I could have a
future in this work.*

(Continued)

(Continued)

Readiness came in stages I think – the green light of readiness to work with clients was arrived at individually – I think I was the third to be allowed that shift. Decisions came from the course director as briefed by one's supervisor and core tutor. Later readiness decisions were mainly a function of group supervision and personal reflection/ challenge – by the end the training was more like a mystery school facilitating initiations and less like a therapy or learning environment.

Qualification was a matter for the whole course team together with outsiders from the Psychosynthesis & Education Trust in London – it mostly felt ok if a bit remote and arbitrary – in that sense it was much closer to my previous experiences of education. For me the qualification made little difference, although I readily accepted it as a symbol of much hard work, effort, expense, energetic invest- ment and sheer bloody minded refusal to give up. It was more a practical matter – will this be recognized in the world and allow me to work? Inwardly I knew I was ready and capable and just needed to accrue more experience and test myself in new situations – the initiation, if you will, was much more meaningful and tangible than the qualification.

Now I feel quite fondly towards it all, though I am much more aware of the limitations of some of my teachers and the perils of a small independent training – such as the enormous multi-hat pres- sure on some of the staff making them less 'available' somehow. I value the training, keep in touch with some of the people I trained with, wish that in a more perfect world that first year had been a bit more integrated and accepting and less loaded with emotional expectation. I also wish there had been an earlier and deeper connection to the rigorous academic tradition – the writings and research fields, although I have made a point of filling that gap post-training anyway. Overall, it changed me and my life, and that is no small matter – embarking upon it was one of the best decisions of my life so far.

I will dig out the course criteria for qualifying; it's in a box file in my attic with all my course papers – is that Ok? From memory it consisted of a requirement for completion of all essay assignments – 6 in all I think, on psychopathology, psychosynthesis itself especially the Will, 2 on specific books – The Primal Wound and another one, also two case studies and I think 150 hours of client experience, plus attendance at all individual and group supervision (weekly, alternating), plus completion of at least 3 years of personal psychosynthesis therapy, and a final complusory retreat.

I think out of an initial group in year one of 25 there were 12 who completed the course and only 4 of us actually went on to practise and make a living as therapists – one of those 4 is now dead so that leaves 3, me and two others. That seems an odd reflection, especially as I know for a fact that my course director was convinced I'd drop out and in fact only accepted me onto the course because they needed the numbers to make the thing viable initially. For me I knew that I needed to do it and once committed, however strange or challenging I felt it to be, I knew I'd finish it – short of failing or being thrown out – it was never a question of giving up or dropping out.

Here again there was some sense of struggle, with the trainers this time, rather than the self. The sense of there being some rite of passage to be undertaken seemed to have been recognized earlier in the training.

Here is the response from the final participant:

At which training organization did you undertake your initial training as a counsellor and/or psychotherapist? *(Information disclosed, but withheld to maintain confidentiality.)*

What was the title of the qualification? (e.g. Diploma in Person-Centred Counselling?) *ABC Diploma in Person-Centred Counselling*

(Continued)

(Continued)

What description of yourself does it entitle you to use? (e.g. Person-Centred Counsellor) *Person-Centred Counsellor*

What attributes were most prized in your training? (overtly or covertly) Who decided? *Being able to offer the core conditions effectively. Fellow students.*

Which were seen as most undesirable? (overtly or covertly) Who decided? *Being judgmental of clients. Being directive in any way. Fellow students during triad work.*

Who decided when you were 'ready'? *Course tutors & placement supervisors who were consulted by tutors.*

Who was involved in the qualification procedures? (People you had previously known, or 'outsiders'?) *As above – people I had previously known and ABC examination board.*

What difference did it make? *None.*

How did you feel about it all? *Was not particularly happy with the student led approach to work in the college. I felt the course lacked structure sometimes and could easily lose focus e.g. Course was easily diverted by people bringing their own individual issues etc in whole class learning time.*

What are you left with now? *Sad that course ended with some friction between certain students as group feedback on each other got very personal and this was not stopped by tutors. I am however very pleased I did the course and feel that overall it prepared me well for the work I have since done.*

Course contents:

Please refer to ABC Level 4 Diploma in the Theory and Practice of Counselling.

- Professional and Organisational Issues in Counselling.
- Counselling in a Diverse Society

- Counselling Theory
- Advanced Counselling Skills
- Self Awareness for Counselling
- Counselling Specialisms
- Counselling Placement.

Conclusions from participants' responses

1 Satisfaction with training experience

While the sample was small and very personal to the practitioner, all the participants experienced some sort of challenge or difficulty. With the first participant it seemed to have been an internal struggle, the second participant's was with the trainers and the third's with other students, and perhaps the trainers. The involvement of trainers is also mentioned in the experience of the first participant. All felt satisfied by what they had gained from the experience, despite (or because of?) the difficulties.

As a profession, we claim that the way to healing and development, and change and learning, is through therapeutic engagement with an other. It is not surprising then, that relationships are what stand out for practitioners from their training. Perhaps being accustomed to coming up against conflicts and difficulties in our training is one of the things that contribute to being able to withstand occasions when we meet it with our clients.

2 Duration of course and theoretical orientation

The second participant disclosed that the duration of the course was three and a half years. The first participant does not disclose the length of the course, but I happen to know that the psychotherapy qualification took seven years. The third participant also does not disclose. It is possible to assume that the course lasted around three years, because that is fairly average.

The orientation of the first participant's course was Humanistic Integrative, the second's Psychosynthesis and the third's was Person-Centred. For the first practitioner the attributes that were valued were 'vulnerability and "not-knowing"'; 'being with' and 'creativity and playfulness. There was an emphasis on the integration of the person rather than the integration of theory. The second participant cites, 'emotional embodiment and willingness/readiness for experiential process individually and in group. I think covertly there was a bias towards engagement with "exotic" practices and life experiences'. The third participant defined 'being able to offer the core conditions effectively' as being most highly valued.

Perhaps inevitably, the theoretical orientation of the course strongly influences what is valued in the student. As an experienced practitioner myself, with some training in all those orientations, I would be able to predict to a certain extent how practitioners might differ. A potential client with no knowledge of the therapy world might find difficulty with understanding the difference. It may also be the case that, while practitioners would understand what their own initial training involved, they would have less awareness of what the training of practitioners from different training providers and orientations had involved. To be able to measure our own competence within the wider profession, it is probably important to have that understanding.

Conclusion

Arising from the foregoing discussions, the principle of:

Acknowledging strengths and limitations of training

is added to the Competency Framework. The Framework so far:

PRINCIPLES OF THE COMPETENCY FRAMEWORK

Cultivation of the self in relationship
Recognizing the impact of difference
Acknowledging strengths and limitations of training

Chapter summary

The nature and range of training available was discussed. The experience of graduates from different training organizations was described. Some similarities and differences in the experiences of the participants were distilled into the third principle of the Competence Framework:

Acknowledging strengths and limitations of training.

ACTIVITIES

Action points

5.4   Write your own answers to my 'research questions':

What attributes were most prized in your training? (overtly or covertly) Who decided?
Which were seen as most undesirable? (overtly or covertly) Who decided?
Who decided when you were 'ready'?
Who was involved in the qualification procedures? (People you had previously known, or 'outsiders'?)
What difference did it make?
How did you feel about it all?
What are you left with now?

If you are still in training then you can reflect on the first two questions, based on your current experience.

PERSONAL REFLECTION

I understand how important it is to standardize and regulate in order for the professions to be accepted by statutory authorities. Individual practitioners will have made choices from a vast range of types of training that are available. Different trainings equip us to be able to do different things. While each of us has something to offer that is valuable, we cannot all do everything everybody else can do. Being competent means being clear about what we can and cannot do.

That being said, I feel a nostalgia for the quirky, creative, occasionally chaotic kind of training I received. Structures and procedures have their place and are important, but if we stamp out idiosyncrasy we become bland. Not only that, if we suppress the 'shadow' then, just like the suppressed aspects of the individual psyche, it will pop up to bite us when we are not looking.

Chapter 6

The competent practitioner

Chapter outline

Tasks and attributes of practitioners that may have particular relevance for competence are identified. The challenges and benefits of being a therapist are defined, and there is a discussion of how work and life impact on each other in therapists' experience.

Introduction

This chapter continues the exploration of the Practitioner element of the Competence Framework by focusing on the experience of practising as a counsellor or psychotherapist over time. While individuals' training and theoretical orientation differ, there is likely to be some commonality in their experience of therapeutic work as an occupation. The chapter begins with a discussion of research that aims to understand how practitioners think and feel about their work. Some of the findings are particularly valuable for approaching a consensus about what being competent might involve. The researchers offer a way of thinking about individuals' involvement with therapeutic work and identify conditions in which it may become problematic. They also identify when work can be satisfying and growth-full.

Continuing Professional Development is generally accepted as necessary for being able to sustain therapeutic work. Our personal and professional lives have a mutual impact on one another, and while work may in itself be an opportunity for development, it can also challenge, make demands and deplete us. These issues are discussed later in the chapter.

What counsellors and psychotherapists do

Orlinsky and Rønnestad (2009) present the findings of a wide-ranging and significant research project into the experience of being a therapist, and how development occurs. A group of practitioners (including the authors) evolved a questionnaire that was based on their own experiences of clinical work. The questionnaire they devised was completed by psychotherapists from a range of nationalities and theoretical orientations, and at different stages of their careers. What follows is a brief summary of some of their findings that are particularly relevant for exploring competence.

Therapeutic goals

The researchers offer a definition of therapy as 'a contractual involvement deliberately undertaken to alter the psychological status of one party' (Orlinsky and Howard, 1987 in Orlinsky and Rønnestad, 2009: 43). The participants were asked to rate the goals they wanted for their clients. Here are their top six:

1 have a strong sense of self-worth and identity;
2 improve the quality of their relationships;
3 understand their feelings, motives and/or behaviour;
4 integrate excluded or segregated aspects of their experience;
5 experience a decrease in their symptoms;
6 develop courage to approach new or previously avoided situations.

(Orlinsky and Rønnestad, 2009: 227)

REFLECTION POINT

What are the positive outcomes you hope for with your own clients? They may be similar or different from those quoted above. Take your list and the research list above. Consider how many of those goals are being met in your own life.

Relationship style

Orlinsky and Rønnestad go on to assert that '[t]he psychotherapist's ability to work helpfully with patients pre-supposes the creation and maintenance of a relationship that is both the context in which the work of therapy takes place and an important healing influence in its own right' (p. 43). For this reason, therapists' relational skills were seen as an important measure of effectiveness. Participants were asked to position themselves in accordance with whether their relational style was warmer or colder, authoritative or permissive. The attributes that were identified as describing the relational style of the responding therapists were, 'accepting (96%), tolerant (91%), warm (89%), and friendly (89%). Many also rated their relational manner as receptive (73%), nurturant (68%) and permissive (56%). By contrast relatively few therapists saw their manner as highly cold (5%), detached (15%), or critical (21%)' (p. 55).

Healing and stressful involvement

Feelings therapists have while being with their clients in sessions were also a subject of the research:

> Items reflecting this aspect of therapeutic work were based on the theoretical and empirical analyses of optimum experience and intrinsic motivation developed by Mihaly Csikszentmihalyi (1990, 1996). Csikszentmihalyi's initial model distinguished three basic subjective states depending on the relative balance of challenge and skill an individual experiences in a particular situation. Feelings of anxiety are expected to the extent that situational challenge exceeds the skills at a person's command. On the other hand, feelings of boredom are expected to the extent that a situation fails to challenge a person's skills. The optimum state of involvement is expected when a situational challenge closely matches a person's skills and demands that they be exercised fully, and at times stretched to new levels. The subjective state characteristic of this situation (referred to as *flow* [italics in original]) is one of intense absorption, finely calibrated responsiveness, and keenly felt satisfaction, generally accompanied by a withdrawal of awareness from extraneous situational cues and a diminution of reflective self-consciousness.
>
> (Orlinsky and Rønnestad, 2009: 45)

Feelings of anxiety and boredom are factors in what is called 'Stressful Involvement'. The description of 'flow' is helpful for knowing when we are working in the most competent way that is currently possible, and is characteristic of 'Healing Involvement'. The need to 'stretch to new levels' shows how important it is to be continually increasing our competence, and that we do so by being involved in our engagement with clients. Of course, we do not work all the time in this way. The intensity is likely to rise and fall naturally. If we never feel that we 'flow' this may be something we need to think about for ourselves, and to talk about with others. Feelings of anxiety or boredom are natural too, and are likely to be experienced from time to time. When we experience either (or both) of them most of the time, it may be a cue to re-evaluate our situation. Continual feelings of anxiety or boredom are likely to cause stress. (For discussions of how to address difficulties that arise see Part II, Chapter 9.)

The factors that contributed to Healing Involvement were defined as being: Theoretical Breadth; Work Setting Support and Satisfaction and Depth of Case Experience. These factors parallel the three elements of the Competence Framework: Practitioner, Client and Context.

- The **Practitioner** has a theoretical understanding with sufficient breadth to be able to make sense of what is experienced in the therapeutic relationship and facilitate movement in a regular, ongoing way. This may be achieved by one initial training, and may be based on a single theoretical model, for example, Person-Centred Counselling. Other training may have a more integrative approach, teaching a range of theories. Practitioners may choose to undertake more than one training. For example, I did a psychodynamic counselling training and then a qualification in Gestalt psychotherapy. I've also done courses in Psychosynthesis, Process-Oriented Psychology and the Jungian approach. Understanding theory at a cognitive level only, is likely to be insufficient for satisfying therapeutic engagement, so practitioners would probably have made a profound integration of their chosen theory within themselves.
- Depth of case experience would involve working with an assortment of **Clients**. This may involve clients from a range of backgrounds with a variety of issues and depths of being troubled. It would involve clients of different genders and age ranges.
- Work Setting Support and Satisfaction is very much about **Context**. See Chapter 8 for further discussion.

The research suggested that Healing Involvement was both satisfying and developmental for practitioners – we grow and develop from actually doing our work. Stressful Involvement could lead to a decline in the experience of practitioners and perhaps towards burnout and Compassion Fatigue. There is a further discussion of Stressful Involvement in Chapter 9 in Part II, which also contains explorations of stress, burnout, vicarious trauma, compassion fatigue and physical illness.

Ongoing professional development

The work itself

Orlinsky and Rønnestad's work was based on an assumption that therapists are vitally interested in their own self-development. Their suggestion that our work is in itself a significant opportunity to develop our selves feels intuitively right. It is also in accord with Buber's (1958/1984) description of the I-Thou encounter in which both participants are changed.

CPD requirements

Professional associations like BACP and UKCP require that their accredited members participate in personal and professional activities throughout their careers. For example, my accrediting association, GPTI, has set a requirement of 250 hours of clinical CPD (including supervision) over a five-year period. I have to complete a record of my activities each year, which is signed by my supervisor.

The specific choice of CPD activity to undertake may be based on the following considerations:

- Making good any deficits in competence identified in clinical work or supervision (see Part II, Chapters 9 and 10).
- Personal interest. The interest may emerge from work with a particular client, or from where we are in our own process.
- Trends in the profession. For example, there seems to be a particular interest in research and neuroscience at the moment. Previously, there has been a focus on trauma or shame.
- What is available within a reasonable area for travel.

Information about training events can be obtained from the periodicals issued by professional associations, for example, *Therapy Today* (BACP) or *The Psychotherapist* (UKCP). Training organizations often run CPD events and it is relatively easy to be on a list to receive emails with details of them.

Professional networks

Much of our work takes place in private. Only we and our clients know what actually happens, and neither of us is in a position to be particularly objective. We cannot decide for ourselves whether we are competent or not in a conclusive way. That judgement has to come from a consensus of our trainers, supervisors and colleagues, and in being seen to meet the requirements of our professional associations. When we attend CPD events and conferences we are allowing our selves to be seen by other practitioners; the response we receive from them gives us a more accurate picture of where we are in our professional practice.

Accreditation

My own experience of becoming accredited, and my support of super-visees undergoing an accreditation process has emphasized to me how important accreditation is as a 'rite of passage'. It is significant because we are required to make some sort of statement of ourselves as a practitioner, to the community in general but also, more importantly, for ourselves. Establishing ourselves as being a counsellor or psychotherapist empowers us in our work. I have noticed that this is particularly important for people working in private practice, where it is necessary to attract clients.

At the moment it is possible to practise without being accredited. It is likely that this will not remain the case long into the future. We may need to make choices as individuals, and as a group, about the kind of accreditation and validation processes we want. Being active in the various professional associations gives us a voice in that decision making process.

Impact of therapeutic work on the practitioner

Being a counsellor or psychotherapist means having support and encour-agement, as well as a context in which to develop and grow. It also exposes us to the possibility of becoming depleted. The empathy we offer our clients that contributes so much towards the creation of a healing environment can lead to over-identification with their pain. Continual giving without suffi-cient replenishment can leave us empty (see Part II, Chapter 9).

Some smaller, but significant hazards include the following.

Ambiguous professional loss

Ambiguous professional loss (Skovholt and Trotter-Mathison, 2011: 120) is where clients fail to turn up for an appointment and then we never hear from them again. There have been situations where this has happened to me and I have left telephone and email messages and even written letters to try and make contact. Coming to terms with when someone 'disappears' has always been difficult. A variant on this is where a client decides to bring our sessions to an end when I know that the work is incomplete. I can let the client know my reasons for believing the work is unfinished, but I cannot make them stay if they insist on going. I feel happy to say goodbye when a client has finished as much as they need to do: that is where much of my job-satisfaction is to be found. I feel a sense of loss, but I know it is the right time for them to go. When the ending is premature, I feel as though everything I have invested in the relationship (and therapists usually invest a lot) has been for nothing.

I can be left feeling frustrated and bitter. The remedy I have found, predictably, is to take it to supervision.

Boundary management

Inevitably, some of my clients are interested in the same kind of topic that I am. There have been several situations where I have turned up to an event to find a student, supervisee or client was also attending. In some contexts that is to be expected: CPD workshops, professional association gatherings or events connected with training organizations with which I have been involved, and can be thought of in advance. When I see clients in a shop, or at a workshop on a topic unconnected with therapy I feel responsible for managing the situation. If I meet a current client, I find that is the most difficult occurrence for me to deal with. Generally I avoid situations where I might meet clients. This means I choose to deprive myself of things I might like to do.

Impact of current life experience

While being a therapist affects our lives, our lives have an impact on our work. Examples are:

- New insights we have gained from our personal work increase our awareness of clients' issues.
- CPD workshops and other training, even if not directly therapy related, can sensitize us to certain aspects of experience. A recent Neurobiology training I attended, facilitated by Barbara Dowds, introduced me to the work of Jaak Panskepp (2006). He identified the basic human emotions and included 'seeking' as one of them. I was surprised, but it made intuitive sense to me. Perhaps seeking is the underlying motivation for the human desire to develop. This new understanding changed my thinking about my own way of being, as well as that of my clients.
- Loss and change. I had been practising for many years before I experienced the death of someone close. I knew about the loss of important people and significant hopes and opportunities but until my parents died I did not know how, and whether, that kind of loss would feel different.
- When physical changes are noticeable by clients: pregnancy; injury; menopausal hot flushes; even a different hairstyle. Decisions around self-disclosure are significant; sometimes we have no choice. We

find ourselves dealing with our own feelings about what we are revealing alongside exploring those of our clients.

Chapter summary

Counsellors and Psychotherapists are interested in their own development as well as that of their clients. The work itself is a vehicle for development, and the requirements of professional associations for CPD contribute to a culture of personal development, and the building of competence levels. Some everyday ways that the nature of the work can deplete and be challenging for practitioners were identified and discussed.

PERSONAL REFLECTION

While I was writing the section in Chapter 3, concerning the practitioner's family of origin, I had a dream about the client I mentioned in Case Study 2.1, the person with whom I had experienced a difficult ending. In the dream she was standing in the garden of my parents' house and sobbing because her aunt had died. She was clutching a white shirt that had just come off the washing-line to her body and hiding her face in it. I don't often have dreams about clients and was intrigued, particularly as several months have passed since we ended our work. One of the Gestalt approaches to dreams – that favoured by Perls – is to assume that every character and object in the dream is a projection of the dreamer's psyche. Which means that I am the garden, the ex-client and the shirt. The atmosphere of the dream was grief for a devastating loss. Maybe some residual feeling about the client (and probably other losses) was being expressed. I certainly felt very bright and positive when I woke up. I also wondered whether the sense of loss that was significantly missing for my client at the time we ended had somehow been accessed for her. Maybe there had been some shift in what Jung called the collective unconscious. It is likely I will never know and, somehow, I can be content with that.

Chapter 7

The influence of the client on competence

Chapter outline

A differentiation is made between the ordinary struggle and not-knowing that is fundamental to the nature of therapeutic work, and circumstances where there might be a barrier to working with a particular client. Some potential barriers are defined and, where appropriate, suggestions are made for addressing them.

Introduction

This chapter explores the Client Element of the Competence Framework. Competence is relational. The people with whom we work, whether they are clients, supervisees or students, have a profound impact on our ability to be competent. Intersubjectivists Stolorow and Atwood emphasize the impact each of us has on the other when they talk about the 'myth of the isolated mind' (2002: 19). Taking strong issue with Basch's (1988) defining of competence, they write:

> According to Basch, the prime motivator underlying all psychological activity is the quest for *competence* (emphasis in original). Which he defines as 'the brain's capacity to establish order among the disparate stimuli that constantly bombard the senses ... *no-one can give you the experience of competence: one must achieve that for oneself*' (p. 27 emphasis added) ... This curious doctrine specifically denies that experiences of competence and self-esteem derive from interpersonal transactions pertaining to one's sense of oneself in the human community.
>
> (Stolorow and Atwood, 2002: 19–20)

For the purposes of this discussion, I will use the word 'client' to represent supervisees, students and any other categories of people with whom we work. Clients can never be 'wrong' in the sense that it is their 'fault' if we cannot work effectively with them. Conversely, it is unreasonable to expect that a practitioner can be competent with every client. Knowing in advance that we are likely to find certain clients difficult helps in dealing with situations that could be potentially problematical. Courses of action can be put in place, like having a list available of other practitioners to whom individuals can be referred. Doing so helps keep both participants safe and, as a consequence, supports ethical practice.

It is important to differentiate between the inevitable failures and mis-attunements that happen in therapy, and a serious breakdown in the work. The following discussions will offer possibilities for understanding what might be happening between practitioner and client in the moment, and help in making that assessment.

The turbulent nature of therapy

Engaging with another person at a profound and authentic level inevitably surfaces difference: world-views collide, sometimes dramatically. While there may be a significant degree of understanding, there will also be misunderstanding. If difference and misunderstanding can be held and resolved, then it is likely to go well. Avoidance of conflict and the impact of difference, is likely to make the work superficial. The skill for the practitioner is to know how and when difficulties can be addressed. Making the wrong decision may mean that the client leaves and never comes back. Modalities each have their own way of conceptualizing what happens in the therapeutic encounter.

In the Person-Centred Approach, the skill is likely to be thought of as holding the balance between Congruence (the practitioner's world-view) and Empathy (the client's world-view) within a pervading atmosphere of Unconditional Positive Regard offered by the practitioner. The practitioner's empathic sense allows them to know when the disharmony of difference may be unbearable for the client. Experiencing the core conditions consistently supports the client to be able to engage in the therapeutic relationship in a more authentic way (Tolan, 2012).

The following quotation directly concerns Kohut, but is likely to represent a general analytic view.

> But equally influential in the treatment process, as it was understood by Kohut, are the ruptures in the analytic bond that come about through the analyst's inevitable and repeated empathic *failures*. In Kohut's view of the analytic process, it is the *movement* between

these two poles of experience for patient and analyst, between affective attunement and rupture and back to attunement again, that enables the patient increasingly to build up and rely on his own self-regulatory capacities.

(Teicholz, 2001: 179–80)

As a Gestaltist, I would conceptualize it differently: the flow of contact between practitioner and client is an important element of the work. Contact is about meeting in the moment, and is embodied. If a client who has previously seemed fully engaged looks away, then a practitioner is likely to pay careful attention, and may choose to share that noticing (Joyce and Sills, 2010). The Gestalt therapy practised by Fritz Perls in the mid- twentieth century would look very different from that generally practised today. Perls seemed to enjoy the clash of difference, even conflict, and consider it therapeutically helpful (Clarkson and Mackewn, 1993). While difference is still seen as necessary for meaningful contact, modern Gestaltists are likely to be less confrontational and more relational, favouring a Dialogic approach. The German philosopher Martin Büber (1958/1984) identified two particular ways of relating which he called 'I-It' and 'I-Thou'. I-It forms of relating are functional: an example from a therapy situation would be arranging a time to meet next week. I-Thou relating happens when both parties recognize difference, and are somehow able to encompass each other, engaging in a meeting that is equal, timeless and energizing, and where each is changed. It is impossible to create an I-Thou moment, although we can cultivate an attitude to enable it.

CASE STUDY 7.1

Martina was in her early thirties. I was intrigued by the way she would dress, with lots of colourful layers and contrasting patterns. We had been working together for about four months. She had started therapy in great distress about a relationship, had made good progress so far, and often let me know how pleased she was with the way therapy was working out for her. On our scheduled meeting day she rang to say she could not make our session because she had a chest infection. Her voice was croaky and she sounded subdued. I thanked her for letting me know and we arranged to meet the following week. As a matter of course, I contract with new clients that they will pay for missed sessions unless there is a possibility of rearranging them within the same week.

At our next session, Martina apologized for missing the session and said she felt much better. There had been a development in her relationship and she seemed very keen to talk about that with me, so I felt unable to bring up the topic of payment. At the end of the session she paid me for just one week. I reminded her then of our agreement and she blushed, looked uneasy and said she had forgotten. She said she didn't have the extra money with her and asked if she could pay the following week. I agreed cordially. The following week she paid for two sessions.

For the next two weeks Martina turned up for her sessions as usual. On the third week she told me she felt much better and would like to end our work on that day. I was surprised, and shared that with her. She told me again how well things had been going. I felt that, despite the initial changes, there was a lot more work to do. I explained that to her, but she was adamant she wanted to stop. Then I remembered about the missed session. I asked if she had experienced a reaction to my asking her to pay, even though she had been ill. She started to cry and said she had been surprised and disappointed, because it seemed so unlike me. I responded as non-defensively as I could, empathizing with her reaction and affirming that it was a natural way for her to be feeling. I also talked again about my cancellations policy and why it was the way it was. I then explained that ruptures occur in therapy and that the important thing was to stay in relationship and resolve them. I observed that she had obviously found it impossible to tell me how I had hurt her, and asked what I could have done to make it easier. She reflected that (unsurprisingly) this was exactly the sort of dynamic she entered into with her boyfriend, only she was never able to tell him she was hurt or angry with him, she just distracted herself or became distant. Our work continued productively.

Constantly navigating the subtleties of our own and our clients' responses, and negotiating conflicts without smoothing them over, or being blown apart by them are some of the major demands for practitioners. In order to withstand them we work on our selves to develop awareness, sensitivity and robustness.

Barriers to therapy

In this section, I discuss situations in which it might be impossible, or highly problematic, for a practitioner to work with a particular client in a specific context. Situations where therapy is clearly helpful, but may make exceptional demands of the practitioner: working with clients experiencing suicidal feelings, for example, are explored in Chapter 9, Part II.

The following pointers are likely to be relevant for understanding how aspects of the client's situation can influence the work:

- ability to engage in therapy;
- readiness to engage;
- the nature of the client, including the kind of transference processes that might arise;
- the nature of the 'issues';
- cultural difference.

Ability to engage in therapy

Clients may be unable to engage in therapy for a number of reasons. The various modalities have their own views of what this might involve. Here, I briefly introduce ways that Person-Centred, Gestalt and Self-psychology practitioners might approach situations where therapy may be difficult, or even impossible for a particular client. I signpost possible ways of working with fragile clients, while pointing out that there might be severe consequences if things go wrong. It is not within the scope of this book to cover any particular theory in depth, only to offer an introduction to the range of approaches available, and point out why they may be relevant for maintaining and developing competence. Readers are encouraged to re-visit the way that working with fragile clients (psychopathology) was dealt with in their own training. If it was not covered, they might want to consider the impact that could have for their practice.

The *Diagnostic and Statistical Manual of Mental Disorders* is a system of classification that is widely used by psychiatrists and other mental health professionals. It is updated at regular intervals and the fifth edition has recently been made available. This version is known as DSM-5 (American Psychiatric Association, 2013). Some training courses use it as a way of helping their students have a deeper understanding of their clients, and enable them to make informed decisions about the appropriateness of accepting clients for therapy in the context in which they would expect to work. The different modalities recommend texts that explain and discuss DSM-5 in a way that is in tune with their approach. If you are not aware of any that are appropriate for your modality, then maybe your supervisor could suggest one.

Approaches to understanding when therapy might be problematic

Carl Rogers considered that psychological contact is necessary for therapeutic work to take place: 'that they (client and therapist) are, at some level, aware of each other's presence' (Tolan, 2012: 83). Tolan goes on to articulate a way of understanding the circumstances when psychological contact may not be achievable: 'Clients may be unavailable for psychological contact because they are angry, frightened or overwhelmed by what is going on inside them' (p. 86).

A Gestalt approach may also consider availability for, and style of contact as a way of assessing a client's ability to engage in therapy. Understanding when therapy may not be possible, or advisable, is described as being where a potential client demonstrates 'a life issue, a condition or a way of behaving that is particularly challenging for the therapist ... Among those clients are those with psychotic process, self-harming behavior, [and] dissociative or regressive processes' (Joyce and Sills, 2010: 201).

Kohut (1984: 8–10) describes what he calls 'Three Classes of Psychic Disorder'. In his discussion of the first class, psychosis, he describes a person demonstrating 'mental hollowness, but a well-developed peripheral layer of defensive structures'. This description seems a particularly apt and helpful one to me. He considered people with these characteristics to have 'covertly psychotic personality organizations', which I understand to mean that they may seem to be engaging with life in a satisfactory way, but find authenticity and spontaneity difficult. Increasing familiarity with such a person may reveal the fragility on which their life is based. As far as availability to benefit from therapy is concerned, Kohut says,

> I cannot imagine that an individual would submit himself to the dissolution of defensive structures that have protected him for a lifetime and voluntarily accept the unspeakable anxieties accompanying ... the task of facing a pre-psychological state that had remained chaotic because ... in early life he lacked the empathic responsiveness that would have organized the child's world.

He modestly adds the caveat, 'I may simply be describing my personal limits as a psychoanalyst'. Like Kohut, I believe that it is important for each of us to acknowledge that we have limits, and be aware of when we may be exceeding them.

Kohut's second class of disorder, he calls Narcissistic Personality and Behaviour Disturbances. He describes this as being where 'the structuralization of the pattern of the self has remained incomplete … with the result that the self reacts to narcissistic injuries with temporary break-up, enfeeblement or disharmony'. He believes that it is possible to work therapeutically with a person in that situation. For those who may not be familiar with what can be known as the narcissistic character style, here is a brief explanation. A baby needs to feel it is central and powerful. It also needs to have that view of itself tempered and made more conditional. If that does not happen in the family of origin, a child and eventually an adult can have an over-inflated sense of their own worth, which is then easily punctured and deflated. I consider my father to have been narcissistically wounded. One powerful example of how this manifested itself in our lives remains with me from many years ago. By this time I was an adult. The whole family, including children and in-laws, was at my parents' house, gathering to set off for a day out. It was a small house, but there were two living rooms and the family was distrib-uted over both of them. By chance, everyone but my father happened to move into one of the two rooms, leaving him alone in the other. He came storming through, declaring that he would not be going on the day out and went upstairs to his room. The rest of us just looked at one another in bewilderment. I only understood what had happened after years of train-ing. Used to being the centre of attention, when it suited him, our random move into the other room must have felt like being shunned. I imagine he would have felt entirely worthless at the time: utterly irredeemable. I can understand this feeling so clearly because I have felt something like it myself. A considerable amount of my time in therapy was spent healing my own narcissistic wounds – to the extent that it was possible.

The third class of disorder is called Structural–Conflict Neuroses. This is where 'a nuclear self has become more or less firmly established in early childhood but that the self is ultimately unable to realize its creative-productive potential': in other words to build sustaining relationships and undertake productive work. Kohut believes that people in this situation (many of us?) are able to respond to therapeutic work.

Deciding whether a client is able to engage in therapy may require much consideration to arrive at a balanced judgement. Sometimes it is glaringly obvious. Because I work mainly in private practice, I become wary when a prospective client tells me they are involved in the mental health sys-tem, perhaps mentioning a CPN (Community Psychiatric Nurse) or a psy-chiatrist. I usually ask what their experience of it is, and if they have a 'diagnosis'. I explain that they may need more therapeutic support than I can provide and, for some people, more practical help than therapy offers. Where other supports are in place, for example working in an agency setting, therapy may be a useful addition to the services provided. Agencies, educational establishments and employers usually have policies in place to deal with a situation where counselling or psychotherapy is either inappropriate, or needing to be supplemented (see Chapter 8).

The consequences of making a wrong decision can be serious:

> There are clients who can evoke difficult and disturbing responses in the therapist, challenge boundaries and need more strategic thinking and management. These clients ... tend to have global difficulties in functioning, may be in great distress and frequently cause suffering and disturbance to therapists, family and friends.
>
> (Joyce and Sills, 2010: 201)

CASE STUDY 7.2

Patrick and I had a telephone conversation before I agreed to meet him for an initial session. I work at home, so I need to feel confident that both I, and the premises are safe when I see someone new, particularly when the prospective client is a man. He told me he had reservations about whether therapy could help, but seemed keen to try. Our communication on the telephone seemed contact-full. The moment I opened the door to him, I felt uneasy. He was a pleasant looking slightly overweight man in his early forties, with light brown hair and a small beard. I asked him in and showed him to my office. Sometimes a first reaction that concerns me can be resolved as I hear more from the person. With Patrick, I became more disconcerted when almost the first thing he said to me was that he did not want his GP to be informed that he was meeting me. Naturally, I asked why and his answer was evasive. The session did not go well and, before the time was up he became agitated and said he wanted to leave. My response was to feel relieved, and I agreed to bring the session to a close. He offered me full payment and I accepted it. When I closed the door behind him, I felt as though I had reached a safe place after having been in danger. I also felt guilty about having accepted the money. My assumption was that he had been seeing his GP about mental health issues, and believed the GP would not approve of his seeking therapy. As I write this, many years later, I find myself wondering if there had been a forensic connection. I begin to fantasize about whether I had had a lucky escape... Clearly Patrick had a profound effect on me.

ACTIVITIES

Individual reflection

7.1   How do you assess whether a client is able to engage in therapy at the moment?

In supervision

7.2   Review any situations where it may have become clear that clients were possibly unable to participate in therapy at that time. What can you learn from these situations?

Group activity

7.3   Participants share their own experiences of meeting with clients who were unable to engage in therapy at that time. What pointers can you identify to help deal with these circumstances? (At least five.)

Readiness to engage in therapy

A person might take action to enter counselling but may not be fully committed to engaging with the work. Here are some situations that can arise in different work contexts:

- In an employment setting, the person may have been 'advised' by a manager or a member of the Human Resources department to access the counselling provision available in that organization. The employee might feel obliged to follow the advice, although not particularly interested in engaging in counselling. This can happen whether the provision is in-house or through an external provider. Sometimes 'counselling' can form part of a disciplinary procedure.
- In an agency setting, support workers may think it beneficial for a service user to access the counselling provision within the agency. The service-user may allow themselves to be persuaded, but not feel fully committed.

- In education, a student may be advised by a tutor to seek counselling and again be not fully committed.
- In private practice, a person might make contact while feeling determined to take some action to deal with the difficulties they are experiencing. When the time comes to turn up for their session, they lose enthusiasm and either call to cancel, or else fail to arrive.

In any context, a client may agree a contract for sessions and then fail to keep to it, for what could seem like plausible reasons. The circumstances surrounding arrangements to meet may be problematic, for example if a client spends a lot of time working abroad, or becomes ill during the therapy. A client could be prevented from keeping to pre-arranged sessions because of last minute work demands. My response when this happens is to accept it at face value and also to 'wonder' about what the unavailability means. Of course, it is only possible to explore what might be happening if the client actually turns up.

The nature of the client and co-transference

I know there are certain people I find difficult to work with. Often the issues are about power or status, and how the prejudices of the individual are at odds with my own. For example, I find it very difficult to work with men who denigrate women, or women whose priorities are centred around others' needs rather than their own. I am cautious about negotiating a therapeutic relationship with a client whose status seems considerably greater than my own, either in my perception or that of the client. The balance of power in a therapeutic relationship is paradoxical. Parity is an important principle yet I need sufficient authority to maintain credibility and trust.

In order to work competently, it is important to have an understanding of when a particular configuration may be challenging. Exploration of their own family background and personal issues helps a practitioner to build insight around particular limitations. Finding a particular therapeutic relationship difficult does not have to be a reason to avoid it. Challenging our own prejudices and finding a way to deal with demanding power dynamics can be growth-full. Support from supervision is particularly helpful on these occasions, by providing both a context for thinking through possible pitfalls, and for obtaining affirmation and encouragement for staying with the difficulties.

REFLECTION POINTS

1 Which client groups do you find particularly challenging?
2 How do you know if a client is causing difficulties for you?
3 How do you find support for working with clients that challenge your world-view?

The nature of the 'issues'

There may be situations where the particular issue that brings a client to seek counselling may be a problematic one for the practitioner, either permanently or temporarily. For example:

- A client wishes to work on bereavement issues related to the death of his mother. The practitioner's own mother died only a few months previously.
- A client wishes to work on her difficulties with regard to food. The practitioner's daughter is herself struggling with an eating disorder.
- A young man wishes to explore his sexuality. The practitioner has strong religious views against homosexuality.
- A male client wishes to explore the reasons for his becoming violent to his partner when they are experiencing conflict. The practitioner is a woman working in a private practice context.
- A client is suffering from a terminal illness and wishes to come to terms with the inevitability of death. The practitioner was diagnosed with cancer several years previously. As far as anyone is aware, treatment was successful.
- An ex-prisoner wishes to talk about his sexual attitudes to children.

These are examples of only some of the situations where a practitioner might find difficulty working competently, because of the nature of issues that are currently troubling a client. Situations where the client's issues may evoke a response in the therapist do not necessarily have to mean that they cannot work together. It has been my experience that clients more often than not bring issues that mirror those in my own life. Often a practitioner may be unaware of the issue a client is concerned with until well into their first meeting, or several weeks, or months, into the work. Supervision is the usual first source of support if difficulties arise (see Part II, Chapter 10). If the work breaks down, courses of action to take are discussed in Chapter 9, Part II.

Cultural difference

In Chapter 4, I identified a number of categories that are relevant for recognizing the impact of difference. I described how a sense of belonging to any 'minority', or even of not belonging to one, may contribute towards the development of a practitioner. In this section, I discuss various approaches to working cross-culturally with clients, supervisees and students. This is by necessity only a brief introduction and, where possible, I signpost readers to further sources of information. As most work has been done on issues of race, I begin there, and continue with sexuality and disability.

Ethnicity

Littlewood and Lipsedge (1989) offer an in-depth exploration of the experience of 'aliens' who find themselves receiving treatment from psychiatrists in the UK. Into that category they place immigrants from old Commonwealth countries like India and Jamaica, and Eastern Europe. They also include Jewish and Irish people. Readers of Chapter 4 may remember that my own family antecedents were Jewish and Irish. They also point out how the experience of women differs from that of men. They describe how other cultures' religious or cultural practices could be misconstrued as insanity from the point of view of the psychiatrist, who is commonly male, white and middle-class – and not always:

> One psychiatrist we know, an intelligent and compassionate doctor, offered her hand to an Orthodox Jew, brought to her clinic by his family. His bland refusal to shake hands with her was however interpreted as 'catatonic negativism'. This young doctor did not realize that Ultra-orthodox Jews may not have any physical contact with women in case they are menstruating. Even within marriage a husband and wife may not be able to pass an object directly from one to another without first putting it down. This prohibition applies during menstruation until the end of the following week, which is signaled by immersion in the *mikveh,* or ritual bath.
>
> (Littlewood and Lipsedge, 1989:181–2)

They observe that:

> Psychotherapy or 'holistic' approaches are perhaps less innocent, less free of social and political ideologies than is biomedicine; they certainly have the potential to be far more insidious agents of social control than the Mental Health Act … There is, of course, nothing inherently wrong with 'social control': it is the process by which all societies reproduce themselves through inculcating shared values and behaviour. The question is perhaps 'control of whom, by whom, for what end?
>
> (Littlewood and Lipsedge, 1989: 294)

They decline to offer any solutions, explaining their reasons in this way:

> Many of us involved in these issues have been criticized for not presenting a detailed programme of action. In part this has been a recognition of powerlessness. In part it has been a deliberate eschewing of what Michael Foucault (1981) called 'prescriptive, prophetic discourse': 'What is to be done ought not to be determined from above by reformers, be they prophetic or legislative, but by a long work of comings and goings, of exchanges, reflections, trials, different analyses … The problem is one for the subject who acts.' Change occurs through the struggles of the people concerned, not because 'a plan of reform has found its way into the heads of social workers or doctors' (ibid). As Elaine Showalter (1987) remarks in her book on women and psychiatry, when women are spoken for but do not speak for themselves, even the most radical and sympathetic psychiatric theories 'become only the opening scenes of the next drama of confinement.'
>
> (Littlewood and Lipsedge, 1989: 294)

This is a powerful argument for diversity amongst practitioners in the professions of counselling and psychotherapy.

From the point of view of being a white practitioner Ryde, discusses approaches she has found helpful in her cross-cultural therapeutic work. She identifies them as being:

- non-dual awareness;
- intersubjective systems theory;

- dialogic Gestalt therapy;
- the 'participative worldview' of action research.

(2009: 112)

For those unfamiliar with any of these approaches, I will summarize them briefly here. Interested readers are encouraged to engage with the book for themselves.

With regard to non-dual awareness, Ryde writes:

> The most fundamental way of understanding non-dualism is to see reality as the mystics from all religions view the world – as interconnected and undivided – not therefore divided into opposing units. Dualistic thinking, on the other hand, views the world as divided into conflicting camps – something is either black or white, right or wrong, male or female, etc.

(2009: 115)

Intersubjective Systems Theory is described in this way:

> The intersubjective systems theorists like Bateson regard contemporary western society as suffering from an epistemological mistake – that of believing in the 'Myth of the Separate Mind' (Stolorow and Atwood, 1992). These theorists view the self as only existing within a co-created relational context. Their understanding implies a way of thinking which relies on what Reason and Bradbury (2001: 4) call a 'participative world view' in which all in the human (and more-than-human) world exist within a web of co-created relationship.

(2009: 119)

Ryde recognizes how a dialogic approach (Büber, 1958), which, with its emphasis on the 'I-Thou' encounter, is an essential facet of Gestalt theory, underlines the way experience is co-created. She draws on field theory (Lewin, 1952), which is also one of the theoretical bases of Gestalt, to illustrate the fundamental inter-connectedness of an individual with her or his surroundings. A field has certain characteristics (Parlett, 1991), which include uniqueness in the moment and the relevance of every part.

The term 'participative worldview' was coined by Reason (1994, 1998, in Ryde, 2009:120). Ryde comments that, 'those who accept a participative worldview know that *I cannot view any part of the world without myself affecting it'* (italics in original). She asserts that this view is, 'suitable for work across difference in culture, even if one culture is more powerful than the other, particularly as it requires us to question our own assumptions.

Sexual orientation

The issue of sexual orientation particularly needs a separate discussion because, in the past, homosexuality has been seen as a condition that needs to be 'cured' (Davies and Neal, 1996). Even as recently as 2009 it was reported in the *Guardian* newspaper that 'British therapists still offer treatment to "cure" homosexuality' (in Daniel, 2009). Besides this, some religious groups consider homosexual practice to be sinful. For heterosexual practitioners, it is likely that considerable attention might need to be given to working with this particular area of difference.

Clark (1987) offers 12 guidelines for gay affirmative practice:

1   It is essential that you have developed a comfortable and appreciative orientation to your own homosexual feelings before you can work successfully with gay clients.
2   Consider very carefully before entering into a psychotherapeutic contract to eliminate homosexual feelings in your client. Willingness to enter into such a contract implies that homosexuality is pathological and undesirable.
3   All gay people have experienced some form of oppression related to their being gay. The subjective reality of that experience must be brought into consciousness so that it can be worked with.
4   Help your client to identify incorporated stereotypes of gay people and begin deprogramming and undoing the negative conditioning associated with these stereotypes.
5   While working toward explaining the range and depth of awareness of feelings, be particularly alert to facilitate the identification and expression of anger. It is helpful for the anger to be constructively channelled and affection openly given.
6   Actively support appreciation of the body-self and body impulses. Don't be afraid to touch your client as a means of demonstrating that you value and trust physical contact.

7 Encourage your client to establish a gay support system, a half-dozen gay people with mutual personal caring and respect.

8 Support consciousness raising efforts such as gay rap groups, pro-gay reading and involvement in gay community activities.

9 Work towards a peer relationship with your client. The message: you are not a second class or inferior person.

10 Encourage your client to question basic assumptions about being gay and to develop a personally relevant value system as a base for self-assessment. Point out the dangers of relying on society's value system for self-validation.

11 Desensitize shame and guilt surrounding homosexual thoughts, feelings and behavior.

12 Use the weight of your authority to affirm homosexual thoughts, behavior and feelings when reported by your client.

(Clark (1987) in Davies and Neal, 1996: 30–5)

Disability

Reeve offers the description of a 'social model' of disability: 'For most disabled people the real problems, such as losses within work or social life, come from living in a disabling environment, rather than the experience of impairment' (2000: 670). She encourages practitioners to use this model as an empowering one for clients with disabilities. She sees it as the 'cornerstone' of an approach to disability counselling that could, 'empower disabled clients by helping them move away from self-blame for being excluded and to develop a positive sense of identity by challenging their internalized oppression' (p. 680)

Conclusion

While much of the literature focuses mainly on race as the area of difference (d'Ardenne and Mahtani, 1999; Kareem and Littlewood, 2000; Lago, 2006; Littlewood and Lipsedge, 1989; Ryde, 2009; Sue and Sue, 1990), many of these theorists' conclusions may contribute towards gaining an understanding of working with difference generally.

Perhaps working effectively across cultural boundaries can seem daunting. Sue and Sue (1990: 171) acknowledge that:

All counsellors have limitations in their ability to relate to culturally different clients. It is impossible to be all things to everyone; that is, no matter how skilled we are, our personal helping style may be limited. This is nothing to be ashamed of, especially if a counsellor has tried and continues to try to develop new skills.

I believe that, at their heart, psychotherapy and counselling are about the healing and creativity that can be released when two people encounter one another, not despite their differences, but in transcendence of them. Approaches that support cross-cultural counselling are likely to make a contribution towards therapeutic work in any sphere.

The first three principles of the Competency Framework:

Cultivation of the self in relationship
Recognizing the impact of difference
Acknowledging strengths and limitations of training

Are joined by:

Understanding the nature of the client and possibilities for therapeutic relationship

Chapter summary

Possible barriers to practitioners' being able to engage therapeutically with an individual client in a particular context, or with certain groups of clients were explored. They were defined as being:

- ability to engage in therapy;
- readiness to engage;
- the nature of the client, including the kind of transference processes that might arise;
- the nature of the 'issues';
- cultural difference.

Where appropriate, possible approaches to addressing the barriers were offered. Readers were encouraged to identify the client groups that are potentially problematic for themselves. A principle was added to the Competence Framework:

Understanding the nature of the client and possibilities for therapeutic relationship.

ACTIVITIES

Individual reflection

7.4 Review your experience of working cross-culturally. Do you have significantly more experience of working with clients from particular categories of diversity? Are there people in some categories with whom you have had no experience of working? Are you aware of any particular personal strengths or weaknesses? Journal for 15 minutes.

In supervision

7.5 With your supervisor, discuss the work with cross-cultural clients that you have explored together. Are there particular patterns that you notice?

Group activity

7.6 Group members stand in the middle of the room. Moving from individual to individual, ask questions to identify who is culturally most like you, and who is the most different. At the end of the process, without disclosing your answer, collect on a flip-chart the various questions used by all the participants in order to carry out the task. Discuss. Finally, disclose 'answers' and notice to what extent they match up, or not.

PERSONAL REFLECTION

At the viva which formed part of the accreditation procedures for my training organization, the first question I and many of the others were asked was, 'Which clients would you not agree to work with?' In those days, a high proportion of graduating students were in private practice and the examiners are likely to have felt that

(Continued)

(Continued)

the answer to this question would reveal prospective graduates' attitude to keeping themselves safe. I guess it might also expose quite a lot about us as people too! I don't know whether I was well-trained, or just lucky, but I've managed to have worked for twenty-something years without coming to grief. That's not to say that there have been no problems. Like most of us, I have been shaken to the core by what has been required of me. I think when I eventually learned to stop wondering what the client was doing that got in the way of progress and look at what I was doing, that things went better. I was taught about three different possible client categories: psychosis, disorders of the self and neurosis. I was told that I was likely to see people who came under the last two categories. I think I see quite a high proportion of people with disorders of the self, particularly with narcissistic processes. This could possibly be on account of my own background and experience. Maybe because I am just sensitive to it. Certainly the combination of my own narcissistic wounds and those of my clients were where I most became unstuck in the early days.

Chapter 8

Context

The significance of setting

Chapter outline

The third element of the Competence Framework is Context. This section examines the impact for therapeutic work of the situation in which it takes place, and how context can enhance competence or undermine it. A range of possible settings is discussed, for example a voluntary agency, the NHS or private practice. Whatever the setting, the administrative arrangements and policies and procedures in place contribute to the effectiveness of a therapeutic meeting. The most significant aspects of these are explored, and sources of further information are offered. Factors concerning the physical space – the building and, particularly the room in which therapy takes place – are highlighted. The possible influence of the social and political context is outlined, particularly the impact of environmental issues.

Introduction

The setting in which a piece of therapeutic work takes place has implications for competence. What would be competent in a hospital or agency setting might not be so in private practice. The features that contribute towards creating a particular context are:

- the nature of the organization and its structure and culture;
- relationship of practitioner to organization;
- policies and procedures;
- the physical space;
- social and political context.

Nature of the organization and the relationship of the practitioner to it

Many people may use counselling or listening skills in their work. Here, I am discussing contexts in which a therapeutic frame is offered to users of the service: weekly or fortnightly sessions lasting 50 minutes or an hour and an explicit understanding of the number of sessions that are available.

The types of organizations within which counsellors and psychotherapists commonly work with this model are:

- private practice as a sole practitioner;
- private practice within a group of practitioners;
- an agency funded through the voluntary sector;
- schools, colleges and universities;
- GP practices;
- other NHS contexts;
- specialist Employee Assistance Providers (EAPs);
- other employers in the private sector.

Private practice

In this context practitioners are responsible for generating their own clients, providing a physical space in which to meet them and deciding how much to charge. Practitioners may work from home, in rented space independently, or at a centre, maybe one specializing in therapy, or perhaps among complementary practitioners. There are clinical issues around providing an appropriate service to clients, and also business issues: how to meet the statutory requirements placed on all small businesses, and how to make enough money to be able to sustain the practice.

Some practitioners join together at shared premises to meet clients. They often provide additional services like training, coaching or consultancy. They may employ reception or other staff and so have to manage statutory requirements in relation to that. Again, enough revenue has to be generated to cover costs and provide incomes for those involved.

Supervisors are chosen and paid by individual practitioners.

Voluntary agencies

A whole range of voluntary agencies offer counselling, either as a dedicated provision, or among other services. They may specialize in a particular type of support, like Cruse and bereavement, or be available to a more general client group. Often, it is in this context that trainee counsellors and psychotherapists have their first experience of client work outside their training courses. In these situations, the work is voluntary and unpaid. In return, students often receive free supervision and other support. Agencies may offer paid work to volunteers at a later stage, perhaps when they have qualified. Supervisors are likely to be provided by the agency and may be paid or unpaid.

Schools, colleges and universities

Universities commonly have a counselling service among the other supports that are offered to their students. Staff there are usually salaried employees, although voluntary placements may be offered to trainees on counselling and psychotherapy courses. The managers of the service are embedded in the university management structure, and there can be opportunities for counsellors to progress to management roles.

At FE colleges, students are less likely to be facing the challenges of living away from home and the provision of counselling support may depend on the circumstances at individual colleges. Some staff may be paid, others there on a voluntary placement.

School counselling is relatively new and pupils may experience a variation in provision.

Supervision is likely to be paid for by the organization, but may come from independent supervisors practising outside it.

GP practices and other NHS contexts

The provision of counselling through the NHS is different in the various parts of the UK. In England Improving Access to Psychological Therapies (IAPT) is the first point of call for patients/clients with anxiety and depression, and is accessed via GP practices. The provision of counselling in GP practices in Wales, Scotland and Northern Ireland is likely to depend on the area in which you live. Supervision is likely to be provided 'in-house'.

Employee assistance provision

Some employers have an internal provision for staff counselling, others prefer to contract the work out to specialist EAP companies. If there is an internal provision, then staff are likely to be employed, and embedded within the organization's management. They would be provided with premises from which to work and would usually have arrangements for supervision made through their employer.

Specialist EAPs recruit associates in areas of the country where they have, or may be seeking contracts with different employers. The associates are responsible for providing premises in which to meet with clients, and possibly for their own supervision arrangements, in return for a sessional fee. Some EAPs provide telephone supervision for associates from employees at their premises.

Requirements in all contexts

The accrediting organizations and codes of ethics

Whether they are employers, agencies or private practitioners, providers of counselling and psychotherapy services do their work within a wider context. One important aspect of the wider field for all providers is the professional organization that provides the code of ethics to which practitioners adhere and oversees procedures for dealing with complaints and applies sanctions where necessary. These may be BACP, UKCP, BPS or an equivalent.

Insurance

Professional Liability insurance may be arranged and financed by an individual practitioner or be provided by an employer or agency. In organizational settings premises insurance is usually provided by whoever is responsible for the buildings. Private practitioners are likely to be responsible for making their own arrangements.

Policies and procedures

The existence of organizational policies and procedures can be very helpful for maintaining competence, and knowing how to deal with situations when competence is exceeded. They are likely to vary according to context, but cover the following situations:

- a client is seriously considering suicide;
- child protection;
- administrative arrangements.

Suicide policy

One of these is likely to be in place in any context for therapeutic work. Even sole-practitioners would, hopefully, know in advance how they would deal with suicidal clients. Larger organizations would have policies that direct practitioners about how to respond. This may involve referral to another service or contact with the client's GP. They are also likely to advise practitioners on how to keep notes on the client's situation, and their own responses and actions. Being able to show that you have followed the correct procedures can help a practitioner to demonstrate their competence for working with vulnerable clients. It is to be hoped that organizations would also have systems in place to support practitioners whose clients have taken their own lives. Such circumstances can be when we risk ourselves emotionally to the highest degree.

Child protection

Practitioners in statutory services are required under The Children's Acts 1989 and 2004 to disclose a situation where a child is in danger. In other contexts, there are strong reasons for also adhering to this requirement (Bond, 2010: 161). Organizations would be likely to have their own policies and procedures for dealing with such a situation, and for keeping a record of how it was dealt with. Where it is mandatory to break confidentiality in these circumstances, some practitioners tell their clients what would happen if a child-protection issue is disclosed before they even start working with them. BACP Information Sheet G18 *Recognising and Acting upon Child Sexual Abuse* (Peden, 2010) may be a useful resource.

Administrative arrangements

The practical procedures that surround therapeutic work can be an important support for the therapeutic frame, as well as making life easier for both client and therapist. The transition from daily life into the room where therapy will take place, and from there back to the outside world can be a significant one. Arrangements are likely to be different depending on context. There may be reception staff to greet a client, and the quality of that contact is likely to set a tone for the session that follows. If there is a waiting area, confidentiality and anonymity might be important considerations. The client may knock on the exterior door of a dwelling and be admitted by the therapist, and that too will contribute to the nature of the whole experience.

A client needs to know how to reach either a pre-determined contact within the organization, or the individual therapist, in between sessions. The convention may be that this kind of contact is kept to a brief minimum, but there needs to be a way for clients to communicate that a cancellation is necessary and to re-negotiate meeting times. There is also a need for a procedure for notifying a client if the therapist finds it necessary to cancel or rearrange a session. This may be a particular issue for a sole practitioner in an emergency situation, and suggestions for how to deal with it are included in Chapter 9 in Part II.

Agencies and employers might require the completion of outcome measures like CORE at certain points in a sequence of sessions. If they are to be used, it is usual to do so at the beginning of (or before) the first session and at the last session. Discussion of the information gleaned from them can contribute to the process of ending the therapeutic relationship. Anonymised data from these forms can be used as evidence of the effectiveness of a counselling or psychotherapy provision and may be included in funding applications. Practitioners may be wary at first of seeing the subtle skill of therapy reduced to a measurement, feeling at risk of being judged and found not good enough. Organizations are likely to discover that, if they are sensitive to practitioners' concerns, then the measures can be both affirming of effectiveness, and a way of identifying areas for personal development. BACP Information Sheet R4 *Using Measures and Thinking About Outcomes* (Roth, 2010) is a source of further information.

Where payment is involved, the client needs to be clear about the amount agreed and the timing and method of payment. Some practitioners expect payment by cash or cheque at the beginning or end of an individual session. Others have arrangements for payment for blocks of sessions and may prefer to have a direct debit or bank transfer in place. Money can be a contentious issue for both client and therapist and having firm structures in place is helpful.

Paper records and recordings

Professional associations, employers and agencies may set requirements for the type of information that is kept about clients, how it is kept, and for how long. There is certain to be a strong emphasis on confidentiality and compliance with the Data Protection Act is likely to inform the procedures.

As an example of the types of notes that are likely to be necessary, here are the requirements of my own professional association, the Gestalt Psychotherapy Training Institute (GPTI):

Records should include:

- client's name address and telephone number;
- client's general practitioner's name, address and telephone number;
- details of client's current involvement with other professionals, including other therapeutic relationships;
- information about relevant health problems;
- a record of the clinical work.

For my own benefit, I collect additional information: details of medication and email details. I ask clients to sign contracts that set out in writing our obligations to one another. I keep notes for at least eight years after the work has finished. The format of written contracts and additional assessment or intake information varies according to context and theoretical approach. Contracting is usually covered in a practitioner's initial training and examples of documentation provided in course textbooks.

Bond (2010: 196–212) offers a thorough exploration of the topic. The BACP Information Sheet P 12, *Making Notes and Records of Counselling and Psychotherapy Sessions* (Coleridge, 2010) is also a helpful resource.

Notes may be requested for legal procedures, or by clients wishing to access the information held about them. It is helpful if there are policies and procedures in place to deal with such eventualities. BACP Information Sheet G1, *Access to Records of Counselling and Psychotherapy* (Bond and Jenkins, 2009) explores this in more depth.

The physical space

By physical space I mean:

- the location and attributes of the building in which therapy takes place;
- the layout of the building;
- the room itself.

Location

The location, and type of building encountered by a client when they arrive for their session send a symbolic message. Individuals are likely to vary in how much of that is in their awareness. Most of my own therapy and supervision has taken place in what look like private houses. In some cases, it was the home of the therapist or supervisor, in others it was accommodation used specifically for their work. Consideration is usually given to a client's confidentiality when entering a building or area. In an organization, if it is possible clients might be seen by others whom they know, then it is considered helpful if they could potentially be on their way to a different destination, rather than be on a route that could only lead to an area where it is known that counselling takes place. Reception staff may provide the initial greeting when a client arrives. It can cause difficulties when reception staff are known personally to clients. People in managerial positions are often aware of how much the arrangements around the counselling room contribute to the overall experience and make sure they are appropriate. When that is not the case, practitioners' competence can be impaired.

Layout

Counselling and psychotherapy take place in private. This means that the accommodation provided must be such that the people involved are neither seen nor heard. Often soundproofing can be a challenge. Hearing a conversation going on in the room next door can be disconcerting for both client and therapist. Being distracted by outside noise, or needing to be vigilant to listen out for the sound of someone approaching makes life difficult for a practitioner and has to influence what they can explore with clients, leading to their levels of competence being compromised.

Access is an important issue, so that clients with disabilities can take advantage of a counselling or psychotherapy service and, especially, that practitioners with disabilities are not excluded.

The practice room

The tradition, especially amongst analysts, has been that the room in which the work takes place contributes to the 'blank screen' endeavour. Consequently, practitioners pay attention to the possible personal nature of the objects they have around them. While I believe that we communicate information about ourselves even if we try to avoid doing so, I would not place personal photographs, or even books other than therapy-related titles in my office. If the accommodation is provided by an employer or a placement agency, there may be fewer possibilities for choice over the content of them: working on a temporary basis in an office that regularly belongs to someone else is an example.

Traditional contents of a therapy room may depend on the practitioner's approach. While 'the couch' is still present in some contexts, more often two chairs of a more-or-less equal height are the usual seating arrangements. Often they are low, softly-upholstered seats positioned at a slight angle to one another. My own therapist favoured folding chairs, like those used by movie directors, placed directly opposite one another and quite close. Other contents of an office might include a desk for writing notes, a shelf of therapy-related books and possibly a computer terminal. A lockable cabinet is an important feature.

Social and political context

Social and political aspects

Attitudes to therapy within communities in different parts of the country are likely to influence the type of service which is preferred. The relative affluence or poverty in an area will also have an impact. Attitudes to therapy in Wales, where I live, are very different from those in Bath, where I work. Bath is generally more affluent than Cardiff and there has historically been a more therapeutically-inclined culture among the inhabitants. Provision of a free service via GP practices, agencies or workplace counselling is gradually making people more aware of how therapy can be helpful. I have worked with clients who chose to finance a longer sequence of therapy for themselves, after having experienced the benefits of a time-limited sequence of sessions in one of those contexts.

The availability of national or local government funding, and the profitability of companies have an effect. In the current recession I have noticed that agencies are losing funding and restricting their activities. I have also noticed that private clients are less willing to travel for therapy because of the cost of petrol. When there is less disposable income, potential clients are less likely to spend money on therapy – at least until their difficulties become unmanageable.

Back in 1993, the provocatively titled *We've Had a Hundred Years of Psychotherapy and the World's Getting Worse*, written by Hillman and Ventura, appeared. Hillman offered the following challenge:

We've had a hundred years of analysis, and people are getting more and more sensitive, and the world is getting worse and worse. Maybe it's time to look at that. We still locate the psyche inside the skin. You go *inside* [italics in original] to locate the psyche, you examine *your* feelings and *your* dreams, they belong to you. Or it's interrelations, interpsyche, between your psyche and mine. That's been extended a little bit into family systems and office groups – but the psyche, the soul, is still only *within* and *between* people. We're working on our relationships constantly, and our feelings and reflections, but look what's left out of that … What's left out is a deteriorating world.

So why hasn't therapy noticed that? Because psychotherapy is only working on that 'inside' soul. By removing the soul from the world and not recognizing that the soul is also *in* the world, psychotherapy can't do its job anymore. The buildings are sick, the institutions are sick, the banking system's sick, the schools, the streets – the sickness is out *there*.

(1993: 3–4)

In the twenty or so years since that was written, it seems to me that the world is continuing to get worse: the environment more polluted, the banking system, particularly, having lost credibility. Seeming to resonate with Hillman, Sanders (2009) asks:

Does theory locate the cause of distress inside the person (their psychology and/or their biology), outside the person (social, material, and economic conditions) or some combination of the two? The location of distress is clearly a political moment in therapy theory and practice. It reveals something of the inherent view of destiny and human nature, and strongly indicates the nature of the 'treatments' endorsed.

(Sanders, 2009: 18)

Perhaps what is being questioned here is whether the values we have as a profession can be kept within the confidentiality of the therapy room, or whether they need a wider arena.

Some practitioners have become particularly concerned about these issues. Understanding the importance of having a voice in social and political agendas, they have developed means for expressing the particular perspective that people who specialize in working with feelings and relationships and, especially with what it means to be human, may have. Psychotherapists and Counsellors for Social Responsibility (PCSR) is one forum that exists for this purpose (see www.pcsr-uk.ning.com).

Environmental issues

In line with concern about the devastating effects human beings have brought about on our planet, interest in Ecopsychology is growing. Totton (2011: 12) affirms the need for, 'an ecosystemic therapy which recognises that humans don't stand alone in the universe, but are profoundly connected with and dependent on other species and entities with whom we share the earth'. Why is this necessary? Brayne (2007: 4) provides a compelling rationale: '[I)] we – I and you … – carry on living and consuming, driving, burning, thinking and just living as we currently do, and do not make massive changes very soon indeed, then human civilisation will end'. The magnitude of this reality is almost impossible to comprehend.

Perhaps a particular challenge for counselling and psychotherapy is to offer some response to the enormity of the dire situation in which we lead our lives (and to which we contribute daily), for ourselves and also for our clients. Environmental activist Joanna Macy offers the cultivation of gratitude as one way forward:

> (O)ur world is in crisis – to the point where survival of conscious life on Earth is in question … There is so much to be done, and the time is so short. We can proceed, of course, out of grim and angry desperation. But the tasks proceed more easily and productively with a measure of thankfulness for life; it links us to our deeper powers and lets us rest in them. Many of us are braced, psychically and physically against the signals of distress that continually barrage us in the news, on our streets, in our environment. As if to reduce their impact on us, we contract like a turtle into its shell. But we can choose to turn to the breath, the body, the senses – for they help us to relax and open to wider currents of knowing and feeling.
>
> The great open secret of gratitude is that it is not dependent on external circumstances. It's like a setting or channel that we can switch to at any moment, no matter what's going on around us. It helps us connect to our basic right to be here, like the breath does. It's a stance of the soul. Gratitude is the kernel that can flower into everything we need to know.
>
> (Macy, 2007: 49)

For further information see: www.joannamacy.net and www.ecopsychology.
org.uk.

CASE STUDY 8.1

Alice arrives early for her appointments; all of them, not just those
with me. She sits in her car and does something useful until it is
time to go to the door. I am always there, waiting to let her in. But
not today. I have been held up and although there are only a few
minutes to go before our session I am not yet at home. Walking
towards my house, I wonder what this unpredictability might mean
for Alice. As I could have foretold, I see her car parked just a little
way up from my house and her figure sitting in it. I wonder what to
do. The strategy I come up with is to wave and gesture 'one minute'
before I go up the steps to my front door. Once inside, I quickly
try and finish my preparations, so I can be ready when the doorbell
rings. I'm too late, and I keep her waiting much longer than usual
before I open the door. She looks uncertain. I smile, try to seem
casual. 'I was held up' I tell her. She takes a breath and walks inside.
About a quarter of the way through the session, I realize she is
telling me about a situation where someone is unreliable and how
difficult she finds that. I ask how it was for her that I may not have
seemed very reliable today. We talk about the situation together,
and I acknowledge the validity of her reactions. We come through
it, and maybe it will be possible for Alice (and me) to cope better
next time.

Chapter summary

These are the characteristics of context that were identified as being
those relevant for supporting competent practice:

- the setting: private practice; voluntary agency; employer;
- policies, procedures and administrative arrangements;
- the physical space: geographical location; layout of building; style
  of therapy room;
- social and political context including concerns related to environmental
  issues.

Factors connected with Context, the third element of the Competency Framework, can be refined into the following principle:

Awareness of context

Which joins with the other principles so far identified to produce the following:

PRINCIPLES OF THE COMPETENCY FRAMEWORK

Cultivation of the self in relationship
Recognizing the impact of difference
Acknowledging strengths and limitations of training
Understanding the nature of the client and possibilities for therapeutic relationship
Awareness of context

ACTIVITIES

Individual reflection

8.1 Reflect on the different contexts in which you have worked with clients. What did they involve that (a) supported you and (b) got in the way of your being competent with your clients? Journal for 10–15 minutes.

In supervision

8.2 What is the context of your supervisory relationship? What aspects contribute to competence, and which potentially form a barrier to achieving it?

Group activity

8.3 Explore your group norms – the unwritten and often unaware 'rules' that you operate under. Which of those contribute to the health of the group, and which undermine it?

PERSONAL REFLECTION

Therapy can be lonely work. Our clients enter our space and leave it, hopefully in predictable ways. A week goes by and they appear again, in the established way to a room that looks pretty much the same as before; maybe a full box of tissues replaces the one nearly empty last time... Something happens. Often that 'something' is rivetingly powerful for both of us. Then the hour draws to a close and we say goodbye. The client steps out into his world, and I stay behind in mine. To sustain myself I need a comfortable, secure space in which to work – and somewhere to escape to in the spaces between clients. I need a reasonable amount of clients and supervisees so that I can make a living. I need the clarity that comes with clear agreements, and I need guidance to deal with situations that might disturb or puzzle me. I need somewhere to take anything I might be left with. All this is context.

Part II

Care of the self

Chapter 9

Highlighting professional self-care

Chapter outline

The chapter begins with identifying circumstances that might indicate competence levels were being exceeded. Possible means of addressing fluctuations in everyday competence are offered, followed by a discussion of contributing factors for stress, burnout, vicarious traumatization, compassion fatigue and physical illness. Suggestions are made for dealing with emergencies that mean we cannot be available for our clients. There is a discussion of the important decisions about when to consider retiring from therapeutic work.

Introduction

Being a counsellor or psychotherapist is demanding. We can spend a lot of our time working right at the edge of our capacity. Inevitably, we sometimes tip over into being outside our levels of competence. How might we know something is amiss?

- Clients complain in a session about the way we are working with them. Of course, this may not actually mean we are being incompetent, but it is a situation that requires close consideration. This is particularly so if more than one client is complaining.
- Clients complain to our professional association.
- Clients miss sessions, or stop coming altogether.
- Clients keep coming but nothing much happens. Again this is part of the nature of the work, but it is worth looking at, and particularly if it is happening with a number of clients.
- The therapeutic frame is undermined in some way: time, or place, or duration of sessions, or difficulties with other contractual arrangements, particularly payment.
- We receive feedback from a supervisor, trainer or colleagues about our work.

- A major event is taking place in our lives, e.g. death, birth, sickness, falling in love, moving house.
- If we are particularly worried about something, like a difficult situation with a family member, money or an impending lawsuit.
- We feel uninvolved, overloaded, stressed, burnt out or ill.

It may be useful here to differentiate between issues to do with everyday competence, and those concerned with more serious conditions. Where everyday competence is impaired, we are likely to be able to identify the 'problem', find a possible solution and implement it. Conditions causing greater concern are those involving stress, illness or burnout.

Remedies for where everyday competence is exceeded

If a concern has arisen, then the following courses of action may be identified as a way forward. I have used the three Elements of the Competence Framework – Practitioner, Client and Context – as structure for the discussion. If the steps to be taken can be discussed and agreed with your supervisor, then they are likely to be more fully effective:

Competence Framework Element 1: Practitioner

Additional personal therapy

I was required to be in personal therapy for the whole of my training (approximately seven years) and my professional association demands as a condition of my practice that I pay attention to circumstance in which I may need to return to therapy. I have done so several times over the course of my career, the last one being a year ago when I needed help to deal with a complicated health issue. The various training institutes have different requirements for personal therapy.

REFLECTION POINTS

How would you know if you needed to enter/re-enter personal therapy?
How would you react if your supervisor suggested you needed therapy?

Further training

There is a whole range of post-qualification training available. Practitioners might want to develop their skills for dealing with trauma, or body process; to specialize with children or other particular groups; work with couples; investigate issues like eating disorders, addiction, dreams and creativity. Certain clients may arrive in our practice and highlight a gap in our knowledge or skills that we pursue further training in order to fill. A look at the back pages of *Therapy Today*, or an internet search will give an idea of what is on offer.

REFLECTION POINT

Is there an area of your practice where you feel under-resourced? For example: working with issues around shame, or using creative approaches?
Ask your supervisor whether she or he believes there is any further training it would be beneficial for you to pursue.

Increased supervision

The accrediting organizations set a minimum requirement for supervision. For example, the BACP sets a standard of an hour and a half each month. There are situations when a practitioner needs additional supervisory support:

- When a practitioner sees her or his first few clients.
- When a client group is likely to bring particularly difficult material, for example victims of torture.
- When a practitioner is working with several demanding individual clients, maybe those considering suicide, suffering from a harrowing bereavement, or with particularly challenging behaviour towards the therapist.
- If a practitioner has lost confidence, perhaps after a long illness of their own, if a client has taken his or her own life, or following a complaint procedure.

The quality of the supervisory relationship is fundamental to dealing with situations where competence has been exceeded. Practitioners need to be able to trust that they will not be judged, but will be supported to regain competence. It is important that the profession encourages a culture that accepts that nobody can be competent all the time, and puts supports in place to resolve situations that occur. A supervisor dealing with a difficult issue with a supervisee, is certain to need consultative supervision for themselves. See the following chapter for more on supervision.

Competence Framework Element 2: Client group

Certain individuals, or even groups of clients may be so challenging, it would be impossible to work competently with them, either for the moment, or in the long term. They may be people who hold views so much in opposition to our own that outrage gets in the way of the ability to be present with them. I had to work very hard on my own process to be able to stay in therapeutic relationship with a client who kept making off-hand chauvinistic remarks. What helped me to carry on was the client's regular and timely attendance at our sessions, upholding the therapeutic frame. If the frame is undermined in any circumstances, then it is more difficult to maintain competence.

It commonly happens that clients who turn up at my practice mirror some aspect of my own process. For example, the week after my mother died a client arrived who wanted to look at her long and problematic grieving process for her father. I thought carefully about whether I could work with her and, on balance, felt I could. A supervisee who had recently suffered a miscarriage found herself talking to a woman who was considering terminating her own pregnancy. My supervisee coped, but it was a difficult session and the work did not continue.

Sometimes a client's current life circumstances are parallel to our own in a way that makes it difficult to remain competent. For this, or for any other reason, it may become necessary to decide not to continue with the work. In my training it was considered perfectly valid not to work with someone just because we didn't want to, and I think that is completely justifiable. A discussion in supervision is a helpful, and probably necessary contribution to the decision making process. You and your supervisor can decide together how to close the therapy and refer the person to another practitioner. Referring clients elsewhere is covered in BACP Information Sheet P17, *Making Referrals* (Walley, 2010).

Competence Framework Element 3: Context

Working in an organization involves following the policies and procedures it has adopted. This can feel like a support and also a constraint.

Individual practitioners obviously make choices about the environment within which they work. Different environments will feel congenial for some and less so for others. That feeling may change over time. Whether they are voluntary agencies or employers, the organizational structure and culture will impact on the experience of the practitioner, and is likely to influence work with clients. In some organizations I have felt valued as a professional, in others I have felt devalued, constrained and bullied.

Clients arrive with pre-conceived ideas about a service that they have picked up either consciously or unconsciously. Where they are limiting or negative, it is likely they may need to be addressed as part of the work, either directly or indirectly. I remember a situation in which I had to find a way of establishing my authority with a status conscious male client. My challenge was to be able to do so without being aggressive, or entering into a competition. I agonized over it in supervision, but with the support of my supervisor, was able to see the situation clearly and move forward. My client and I managed to establish a mutually respectful working alliance. Therapists tend to put the interests of clients before their own, wherever possible. When a work context is uncomfortable, or undermining, practitioners may protect their clients by bearing the brunt of the negativity themselves. This can lead to a practitioner's suffering from stress and burnout.

When a practitioner in an organization is having difficulty remaining competent, it is likely to be more apparent to others than would be the case in private practice. Clients cancelling sessions, less consistent scores on outcome measures, negative feedback or the practitioner's general demeanour are likely to come to the attention of those in a managerial role. Any responses would probably follow general organizational guidelines. It is to be hoped that the special demands of therapeutic work would be recognized, and support put in place. Further training, additional supervision or entering personal therapy (as discussed above) are likely to be the most regularly used remedies. Discussions between the practitioner and the relevant manager would be the likely route for deciding a course of action. The clinical supervisor may also become involved.

Stress, burnout, vicarious trauma, compassion fatigue and physical illness

Stress

The demands of clinical work can result in stress. This may be particularly so when additional factors are involved:

- Unsupportive work environment or organizational attitudes. Possibility of radical change, loss of funding for example.
- Challenging circumstances at home as well as at work.
- If a difficult situation has gone on for a long time.
- Reaching the end of regular cycles that are particularly busy: 'end of term' or similar situations.

General symptoms of stress can include:

- Waking in the middle of the night, or early in the morning, and feeling anxious.
- Feeling overloaded and anything extra to deal with, however small seems overwhelming.
- Impatience, quick to feel frustrated or angry.
- Afraid to take time off work.
- Physical symptoms: aches and pains, tension in shoulders, stomach, jaw etc., exhaustion.
- Increased alcohol intake.
- Inability to relax.
- Feeling hopeless and worthless.

I know when I am starting to be stressed when I experience a sugar-craving, particularly focused at cake. My body seems to be desperately in need of more energy, yet sugar is only a short-term solution that just leads to more craving, and no real satisfaction. Sometimes I have felt so tired that I have to take a short nap between clients. When I notice these things happening, I know it is time for a break, or that something needs to change.

Stressful work involvement

Orlinsky and Rønnestad presented the findings of wide-ranging research into the experience of being a therapist, and, particularly, how development occurs (see Chapter 6 for further discussion). They identified two types of work involvement, distilled from the responses of the therapists they surveyed. They called them Healing Involvement and Stressful Involvement. Characteristics of Healing Involvement were described as being: invested, affirming, flowing and coping constructively with difficulties. Practitioners experiencing Stressful Involvement were described as feeling anxious, bored, frequently in difficulty and wanting to avoid therapeutic engagement (2009: 64).

High Stressful Involvement was associated with therapists feeling Little Work Setting Support and Satisfaction (3%), having no independent private practice (1%) and experiencing little Professional Autonomy (0.4%). Thus, by implication, therapists who feel supported and satisfied in their main work setting, who have a large measure of Professional Autonomy, and who spend at least some time in independent private practice are less likely to experience therapeutic work as Stressful Involvement.

(Orlinsky and Rønnestad, 2009: 76)

The researchers conclude that:

Being as human as their patients, therapists inevitably bring limitations and vulnerabilities with them into therapy. Some of the limitations may be due to the therapist's failings ... whereas others may be due to the enormity of the task presented by the patient's condition or life situation ... In certain situations, these limitations and vulnerabilities may render therapists ineffective and subject them to emotional distress.

(Orlinsky and Ronnestad, 2009: 65)

These observations parallel the three elements of the Competence Framework: Practitioner, Client and Context.

Burnout

If stress signals are ignored for long enough, burnout occurs.

Burnout is the index of the dislocation between what people are and what they have to do. It represents an erosion in values, dignity, spirit and will – an erosion of the human soul.

(Maslach and Leiter, 1997 in Skovholt and Trotter-Mathison, 2011: 148)

The organizational context in which a practitioner works is likely to be a strong contributing factor, because of aspects such as:

- work overload;
- lack of control;
- insufficient reward;
- breakdown of community;
- unfairness;

- significant value conflicts;
- lack of fit (incongruence between the person and the job).

(Mashach and Leiter, 2008: 500–1 in
Skovholt and Trotter-Mathison, 2011:150)

Skovholt and Trotter-Mathison, identify two types of burnout that they call Meaning Burnout and Caring Burnout (2011: 152):

> Meaning burnout occurs when the calling of caring for others and giving to others in an area such as emotional development, intellectual growth, or physical wellness no longer gives sufficient meaning and purpose to one's life. Individuals in the caring professions often derive much 'psychic income' from helping others.

To describe Caring Burnout, Skovholt and Trotter-Mathison refer to what they call the Cycle of Caring (2011: 20). Client work begins with the creation of an empathic attachment, which develops into a phase where the practitioner is actively involved with the client. When the work is at an end, a separation occurs that the practitioner experiences as loss. If the involvement has been intense, then the sense of loss is likely to be powerful too. Multiple attachments and involvements are likely to result in a build-up of what is called 'felt separation'. To recover from this process, the practitioner needs to take time away to rest and be renewed. This is known as the re-creation phase:

> If the inevitable separation with the client … does not too severely deplete the practitioner then he or she can attach again. But if the process drains the person, perhaps each time just a little … then the life force, the blood flow for the counselor … is gradually choked off. This is the caring burnout process.

(Skovholt and Trotter-Mathison, 2011: 153)

Remedies for stress and burnout tend to require a break from clinical work. This need can possibly be met by a holiday, or may necessitate a period of sickness absence. In some organizations, it is possible to take a sabbatical, or extended period of leave after some years of service. Regular breaks, and involvement in meaningful activities other than work are a protection against stress and burnout (see Chapter 11).

Vicarious trauma and compassion fatigue

Vicarious trauma and compassion fatigue tend to be described in a similar way. Compassion fatigue can be defined as, 'a state of tension and preoccupation with the traumatized patients by re-experiencing the traumatic events, avoidance/numbing of bearing witness to the suffering of others' (Figley, 2002: 1435, in Skovholt and Trotter-Mathison, 2011: 146). By allowing ourselves to over-identify with the sufferings of some clients, we may take on their trauma ourselves, experiencing what is known as vicarious trauma. This is one therapist's description of that involvement:

> Prone to over-identifying with clients, I tend to experience much of their emotional pain and internal struggles as if they were my own. The permeability of my ego boundaries may facilitate empathic contact, but it also leaves me vulnerable to emotional overload. Especially when working with more disturbed individuals, hearing and digesting their stories of past and present abuse can be highly disturbing.
> (Sussman, 1995: 21 in Skovholt and Trotter-Mathison, 2011: 134)

If we are preoccupied with certain clients' stories, we are unavailable to resonate with those of others, so we can be said to be experiencing compassion fatigue.

In some ways, compassion fatigue and vicarious trauma are the downside of empathy. When I hear student psychotherapists and counsellors say they are feeling their clients' feelings as if they belonged to them, and telling me as if it were a grand thing to be able to do, I remind them that true empathy involves being able to acknowledge difference. We need to be able to move in close to our clients, but we also need to be able to step away.

Physical illness

Being in private practice I am likely to continue to work through most illnesses. I have carried on seeing clients when my physical condition was such that I could hardly walk to see them in and out of the room. I have known other practitioners act in a similar way. There have been times when I was unable to work following an operation and have had to suspend my practice temporarily. My clients, of course, noticed my deteriorating condition and for at least some of them, it was probably a relief when I finally chose to stop. Despite its conveying a strong work ethic, I am not sure whether I deal with sickness in a way I would like, if I were to think about it. I believe that illness is a message that something in my life needs to change. My experience is that, if I ignore symptoms, they will continue to increase until I give them proper attention.

My own experience of substantial sickness absences was that I knew in advance that they would take place, so was able to negotiate with clients and colleagues in person and in a timely way. That is not always the case. The next section discusses arrangements for dealing with emergencies.

Dealing with emergencies and deciding when to stop for good

Possible emergency situations

While the thought of sudden death is uncomfortable, most of us will go so far as writing a will, so that the possessions we leave behind can be shared amongst our loved ones in a way that we think appropriate. For those of us in private practice particularly, the concept of a 'clinical will' (Despenser, 2008: 31) is a useful one.

Practitioners working in organizations are likely to have systems in place that cover their absence: a designated person would contact clients using details held centrally and explain the situation. The reason for absence may be as simple as a couple of days off with a cold, or an emergency dental appointment, but may involve a more serious long-term absence and even death. Where an absence is likely to be long term, arrangements for referral to other practitioners can be put in place.

That kind of support is not available to sole practitioners. I have made arrangements for dealing with my possible sudden death, incapacity or other unavailability. I keep a list of current clients and supervisees, just first name and mobile phone number, in a prominent corner of my desk. I give clients and supervisees written details of emergency arrangements at the start of our work. I tell them that they will be contacted by someone who knows only their first name and telephone number, but who is able to deal with both their emotional responses and any practical arrangements. My 'clinical executor' is an experienced therapist (and friend) who lives locally. I have shown her my practice room and the arrangements I have for keeping notes. Her contact number is written in red on the list I have on my desk. I have told family and friends the arrangements I have agreed, and shown them where I keep the list. If an emergency were to occur, someone would contact my clinical executor, who would come in and deal with notifying clients. The arrangement I have with my legal executor is reciprocal – I would deal with any emergency situations for her.

I have never had to test the system, but I was very glad it was in place when I had food poisoning a few weeks ago. I woke in the night feeling very ill indeed, so much so that I wondered if I would have to go to hospital. It was a working day the next day and I knew that some clients would be setting off early because of the distance they had to travel to reach me. I certainly felt too ill to be negotiating phone calls with anxious clients, and was worried that my condition would worsen. I resolved to contact my clinical executor first thing in the morning. Luckily, by dawn I felt better and managed to do my day's work. I did wonder about whether I was really taking care of myself by going ahead with seeing clients, but the alternative seemed complicated and as if it would require more energy. This kind of situation is an example of the particular pressures on therapists working in private practice.

The possibility of imminent death may be challenging to come to terms with. Other eventualities that may suddenly strike us down are scarcely easier to contemplate: the loss of a close family member; sudden mental or physical incapacity. If we can face the possibility of these emergencies and have structures in place to deal with them, we will make a significant contribution to remaining competent. We would know that our clients, colleagues and supervisees, our loved ones and, perhaps most importantly ourselves, are held safely in a framework that would support us even if the worst were to happen. That knowledge is a subtle but significant support for competent practice.

REFLECTION POINT

What would happen to your clients, supervisees, students and colleagues if you were suddenly unable to work?

Retirement

Age brings loss of faculties. Gradually, we discover we need to wear glasses, ask others to speak up, and have to ease out slowly after sitting for a long time. We lose a particular word we were looking for, forget names and wonder why we have come in to a room. Age can also bring extensive knowledge and experience, profound understanding, perspective, individuality, equanimity, deep reverence and idiosyncratic irreverence. The changes age brings do not happen to individuals at the same time. As we become older, how do we know that we are still competent to do our work with clients, supervisees and students?

Sugg (2011: 18) offers the beginning of a dialogue. An anonymous contributor to her article observes:

> So counselling is a strange profession in that there seem to be no guidelines for retirement. Age is generally seen to be an advantage in this sort of work rather than the drawback it is for some professions. And who, apart from my supervisor or some well-meaning colleagues will suggest it is time to wind up my career?

Russell and Simanowitz (2013) continue the debate. They comment on research with a group of retired counsellors. Their contributors resigned at different ages and for different reasons. Perhaps that individual choice of time will continue to be the convention: we recognize that the process of becoming a counsellor or psychotherapist involves an individual journey, maybe the decision to stop needs to be arrived at in an equally personal manner. Theoretically, it is possible to continue working into our seventies, and even eighties and nineties. Therapists have usually gathered an enormous amount of self-awareness over time, so may be well placed to understand when it is time for them to stop. Inevitably, though, we all have blind-spots. Establishing a discipline of giving attention to remaining competent throughout our careers will help us avoid finding ourselves in a position where we have gone past the time we really needed to stop. Winding down a practice takes time, so being able to plan for that well in advance is one of the final services we can offer our clients.

I have met people who decide to train as counsellors to give themselves a way of continuing to work and earn an income after they have retired from their current career. I wonder about that. Counselling is sedentary and measured, and there is flexibility about the amount and timing of work undertaken, but it does require an amount of psychic and emotional energy, sometimes a very large amount. A body needs to be fit enough to withstand that. My contribution to the debate, in the form of my thoughts about my own retirement, end this chapter.

Conclusion

The Competence Framework is designed to be a way of assessing moment-by-moment competence on our work with clients, supervisees and students. The three Elements of Practitioner, Client and Context offer a process for decision making that is simple enough to be used in the intensity of therapeutic engagement. Competence is likely to fluctuate because we are human, but it may come to our attention that areas of our work may need further development. For everyday competence issues it is likely that personal reflection or consultation with a supervisor or trusted colleague will point to a way forward that can be implemented, while we continue to carry out our work responsibilities. Certain conditions, like stress, burnout, compassion fatigue and serious physical illness are likely to require a complete break from work activities. Unforeseen emergencies might also make us unavailable to meet our clients. We need measures to be put in place to deal with these sudden occurrences, particularly if we work in private practice. The question of when to retire finally from therapeutic work is one that is important to consider before we have permanently lost our ability to practice competently. Being attentive to competence levels in a routine way may help to indicate if there is a diminishing of our ability. The principle of:

Identifying and remedying difficulties

is added to the Competence Framework. Here is the current list:

PRINCIPLES OF THE COMPETENCE FRAMEWORK

Cultivation the self in relationship
Recognizing the impact of difference
Acknowledging strengths and limitations of training
Understanding the nature of the client and possibilities for therapeutic relationship
Awareness of context
Identifying and remedying difficulties

Chapter summary

Suggestions for ways of addressing competence issues in everyday work were offered using the Elements of the Competence Framework: Practitioner, Client and Context as a structure. Longer-term conditions like stress, burnout, vicarious trauma, compassion fatigue and physical illness were discussed. There was an exploration of arrangements for dealing with emergencies, and preparations for retirement.

PERSONAL REFLECTION

I'm not of an age where I can receive a state pension yet, so a decision to retire is a bit academic because I couldn't really afford it. My father gave up work early and spent a long time seeing his life continually narrowing; until eventually we found he was suffering from Alzheimer's. My intention since has been to keep working as long as I can. Having to re-accredit for the third time this year has made me wonder how long I will want to go on doing the same thing. A part of me longs for something new and, when that is how I'm feeling, I look at the aspects of my life that have the most energy. At the moment, it's this book and the topic of it. I feel I have something to say, and want the community to know what I have learned over all these years. Perhaps writing, and talking about this subject that is so important to me, will take me into another phase of my career.

Chapter 10

Highlighting supervision

Chapter outline

Casement's concept of an internal supervisor is identified as being a step towards both undertaking reflective practice and working in regular supervision, so is essential for explorations of competence. The ways that the different approaches to supervision – training; consultative and peer – facilitate competence to be maintained, and can be the context for any breaches to be remedied are identified and discussed.

Introduction

Supervision is one of the most important contributions to competence. It is where we can bring our disasters and dilemmas, our questions and satisfactions. Our supervisors are likely to know our work better than anyone, apart from ourselves or our clients. If we are fortunate enough to be able to maintain a supervisory relationship over time, then the supervisor will come to know us as an individual as well as a professional.

Although we are likely to meet with our supervisors only once a month, supervision works best if it is an ongoing process. This is encapsulated in Casement's (1992) concept of the internal supervisor. The discipline of Reflective Practice (Schön, 1991) is also essential to the maintenance of competence – if we do not reflect on our work then we miss out on opportunities for understanding that are likely to be valuable. Supervision proper is explored in the third section of this chapter.

Internal supervisor

To illustrate the concept of the internal supervisor, Casement writes:

> Support from a supervisor … can offer *hindsight* [italics in original] on what has been missed in an earlier session; it can also offer *foresight* in relation to what may be yet encountered. Therapists still need to develop a capacity to function with more immediate (but not instant) *insight* within the momentum of the analytic process.
>
> (1992: 30)

He likens the internal supervisor to what he calls the 'observing ego' (p. 31), which is distinct from the 'experiencing ego'. He considers that the observing ego starts to be developed during the practitioner's personal therapy: part of the role of the therapist is to help a client to notice what they are experiencing, as well as being very involved in the experiencing of it. Development of an internal observer helps us to notice when we are about to step into one of our old patterns and to avoid it (although perhaps not always).

Hawkins and Shohet:

> believe that supervision begins with self-supervision: and this begins with appraising one's motives and facing those parts of ourselves we would normally keep hidden (even from our own awareness) as honestly as possible. By doing this we can lessen the split that sometimes occurs in the helpers, whereby they believe they are problem free and have no needs, and see their clients as only sick and needy. As Margaret Rioch (Rioch et al., 1976) says: 'If students do not know that they are potentially murderers, crooks and cowards, they cannot deal therapeutically with these potentialities in their clients'.
>
> (2006: 5)

While they explain it slightly differently, both Casement and Hawkins and Shohet affirm that a process of self-exploration is necessary for an individual to develop a sufficiently adroit observer self. Unsurprisingly, being able to stay within our levels of competence in our work also requires a process of self-exploration to hone the observer.

Using the internal supervisor

Casement (1992) offers some examples of how he uses his own internal supervisor. One of them he calls 'Trial Identification', which involves purposely imagining how a client might feel hearing what it is he is about to say. Casement writes:

The capacity to be in two places at once, in the patient's shoes and in one's own simultaneously, can only be encompassed if therapists can develop a capacity to synthesize these apparently paradoxical ego states. It is here, I believe, that the processing function of the internal supervisor comes to the fore. It is more than self-analysis and it is more than self-supervision.

(1992: 35)

Casement offers a detailed explanation of how he uses his internal supervisor to frame an interpretation (p. 42). Those of us who practise from a perspective other than an analytic one would use it differently. One of the situations that I find needs deep consideration is where a client would like me to tell them what I think about a decision they must make:

CASE STUDY 10.1

Lucy is in her mid-thirties with two young children. She and her husband are not getting on and she is considering ending the relationship. Money is tight in the family and it is a stretch for her to afford to pay for our sessions.

Lucy: My mother wants me to bring the children and go and stay with her for a while.

Gerrie: Is that what you want to do?

Lucy: I'm not sure. (Lucy bites her lip).

At this point I am aware that Lucy would probably like me to tell her what to do. She understands that I probably won't do that because she has some knowledge of what happens in counselling. I know from previous sessions that her mother, who lives fairly close by, often tells Lucy what to do, so it is no surprise to hear that she has made this suggestion. One of the difficulties Lucy has been experiencing with her husband is his criticism of her for being unable to make even simple decisions.

My thinking about Lucy is that she indeed does not know what she wants, because she has had to deny her feelings and desires from a young age. I consider it would be helpful for her to regain

(Continued)

(Continued)

connection with those sensations and emotions so that she could eventually learn to know her self again. First of all, I believe she needs somehow to give herself permission to re-connect.

I have several choices here:

1   Suggest that at some level she would like, or is expecting that I will tell her what to do.
2   Say how difficult it probably was for her to have all that pressure on her.
3   Ask if she would like us to identify some 'fors' and 'againsts' going to stay with her mother.
4   Draw her attention to what is happening with her lip.
5   Wonder if she could come up with an image that illustrates her experience.
6   Disclose my own feelings of sadness for the child who had to stop herself having feelings in order to deal with her situation.

Reflection points

What other interventions might be possible and helpful at this point?
What would be the most likely intervention from your theoretical orientation?

'Lucy' is a composite of many clients with similar issues that I have met. Which intervention would be most helpful? Well, I've used all of them many times, in many situations with all sorts of different responses. What is true for all of them is that there would be a theoretical rationale for using them. Intervention 1 might come from a more psychodynamic perspective with a focus on transference; intervention 2, an empathic response from the Person-Centred tradition; intervention 3 would be a more cognitive style; intervention 4 relating to embodied approaches (including Gestalt); intervention 5, transpersonal, Jungian etc.; intervention 6, dialogical Gestalt and the Intersubjective.

Some considerations for making a choice might be:

• **Cultural influences.** Lucy is a white western woman. My perception of this culture is that women are often brought up to be deferential; to sacrifice their needs for the benefit of others. With moves towards gender equality, expectations change and she may be living through that dilemma in her relationship. Had she belonged to a more collectivist culture (see Chapter 4), then I would allow those different cultural expectations to inform me. Had she been a man, I would have wondered about shame issues.

- **Stage of the work.** The work with Lucy is near its beginning. She is unaccustomed to therapeutic work. My previous experience tells me that it is difficult for some clients to believe that the care they received from their parents might have been hurtful for them. In this situation, I would want to avoid any suggestion of blame against Lucy's mother.
- **Client's way of working.** Some clients easily connect with their bodies and find body awareness work helpful. In this situation, I think Lucy might have felt criticized, been embarrassed, or even shamed, if I had mentioned what was happening with her lip. If Lucy had used visualization CDs herself previously, and we had done some image work together then that might have influenced my choice.
- **Stage of the session.** If we were approaching the end, I might assess the possible strength of Lucy's response and allow that to inform me. It is likely that identifying two to three 'fors' and 'againsts' might not take very long, and would be less likely to evoke powerful emotion than if I disclosed my own feeling or empathized deeply with hers.
- **My felt-sense.** While it is possible to analyse possible interventions in a rational way, there is something about being flesh and blood in a room together, with only the encounter itself on which to focus, that engenders its own imperatives.

Using the internal supervisor/observer self

My choice of intervention in the moment would have evolved from my individual life-experience, understanding of diversity, knowledge of theory, the nature of the relationship I had formed with my client, and the wider context within which the work was taking place. I would not have had time to surface my thought processes in the way I have described here. I can conceptualize the process that takes place by using the gestalt theory of figure and ground (Joyce and Sills, 2010: Zinker, 1978). Gestaltists believe that human beings make sense of the world by organizing our experience in a particular way. One aspect of our here and now experience comes to the fore, while everything else slips into the background temporarily. It's like seeing the face of the person you've been waiting for emerging from the crowd. Great artists know how to use this: look at any picture and your eye will immediately be drawn to the point the artist wants us to make significant. Noticing what is 'foreground' for me, and framing an intervention around it is practically instantaneous. I can reflect on a situation and allow the background detail to come into focus, as I have here, but that would distract me from being immersed in engaging with my client. In a session I move between being fully immersed and being reflective, in a rhythmical way – and sometimes not so rhythmically! This reflective capacity is my internal supervisor, or observer self.

Because I know well that, 'the meaning of a transaction lies in the communicative space *between* [italics in original] the dialoguing partners' (Clarkson, 1998), once I have made my intervention, I will be watching and listening closely to see how my client responds to it. When the response has been conveyed, my figure-making cycle begins again.

Conclusion

In this section I revisit Casement's description of the Internal Supervisor, a concept which is familiar to most of us. My case-study example describes how, in a session with a client I can move between being fully immersed in the experience and momentarily step outside it in order to reflect on it. I show how I use my own Internal Supervisor, or observer self to reflect on my work with a client both while it is taking place, and afterwards. My observer self helps me make choices that establish my competence, and also with recognizing when I am stepping outside my area of competence. It can do that work in the intensity of the actual session, or at a later stage.

No doubt readers will be able to pick up on aspects of the case study that are outside my current awareness. By inviting you in to my experience of working with a client, I reveal gaps in my awareness that you can pick up on because your point of view is different from mine. This is a simplified definition of supervision. We will go on to look at supervision more closely later in the chapter.

ACTIVITIES

Individual reflection

10.1 What is your own process for choosing particular interventions? Perhaps allow your 'observing ego' to inform you as you work with your clients. Journal to explore how much of your decision-making process is associated with thoughts, feelings, body sensations or intuitions, or a balance of some or all of them.

In supervision

10.2 Choose a short exchange between a client and yourself (or even just one 'interesting' intervention) and discuss how you chose to say what you did, and what else you might have done in that situation.

Group activity

10.3 The facilitator, or a group member leads a visualization. Grounding and focusing as a lead into: 'This is a visualization to explore your observing ego. Connect with your breath. Watch the flow of cold air in through your nostrils, notice your body fill with breath, then allow it to trickle away, noticing how it has become warm now. Who is observing your breath? Connect with the part of yourself that is noticing your breath. Maybe you have some thoughts now? Notice that you are thinking, but do not become involved with the content of your thoughts. Who is observing your thoughts? Stay with this for a few moments, noticing your breath, and noticing your thoughts...' Come back to room and make a drawing. Share drawings and experience.

Reflective practice

In his book *The Reflective Practitioner*, published originally in 1983, Schön takes as his starting place the realization that traditional ways of learning were inadequate for practitioners working in situations where, 'complexity, uncertainty, uniqueness and value-conflict' (1991: 39) are the norm. He came to the conclusion that because, 'competent practitioners usually know more than they can say' (p. viii) and while 'the art is not invariant, known and teachable, it appears nonetheless, at least for some individuals, to be learnable' (p. 18), then an approach involving 'reflection-in action' (p. ix) might be valuable. Schön writes:

> When we go about the spontaneous, intuitive performance of the actions of everyday life, we show ourselves to be knowledgeable in a special way. Often we cannot say what it is that we know. When we try to describe it we find ourselves at a loss, or we produce descriptions that are obviously inappropriate. Our knowing is ordinarily tacit, implicit in our patterns of action and in our feel for the stuff with which we are dealing. It seems right to say that our knowing is *in* [italics in original] our action.
>
> (1991: 49)

Reflective Practice is about bringing into awareness what is implicit in our actions: 'There is no absolute knowledge; knowledge develops all the time through interaction between people and their environment' (Bager-Charlson, 2010: 16). By reflecting on what we do, we can distil the new learning that has taken place as a consequence of going about the everyday tasks involved in our work with clients.

Schön observes that:

> A practitioner's reflection-in-action may not be very rapid. It is bounded by the 'action-present', the zone of time in which action can still make a difference to the situation. The action-present may stretch over minutes, hours, days, or even weeks or months, depending on the pace of activity and the situational boundaries that are characteristic of the practice.
>
> (1991: 62)

In one sense, the practice of counselling and psychotherapy takes place over weeks, months or years, depending on individual clients. In another sense, it lasts for an hour: the face-to-face weekly session. It makes sense to use reflection-in-action to measure competence both during the session, as described in the previous section, and at other times within the life cycle of a particular piece of client work. Many of us take time after a session to reflect on it, either directly after the session or some time later in the day, or over the next few days. Supervision is an example of scheduled, dedicated time to reflect with another person.

The Reflection Points included in the chapters of this book are invitations to engage in Reflective Practice. Thinking about a situation and, particularly writing about in an uninhibited way, bring new insights. We can take the exploration to a deeper level. Bager-Charlson, (2010: 13) writes: 'Reflective practice prompts questions about *what* we know and *why*, i.e. how we come to know it.' For example, in Case Study 10.1 in the previous section, I made a list of possible interventions I could choose from to respond to Lucy. Why did I arrive at that particular list? Using the elements of the Competence Framework to help me explore, I will look at the influence of Practitioner, Client and Context. Here, I will begin with the element relating to the client.

- The **Client** told me herself that she had difficulty making decisions, and I had noticed for myself that was the case.
- The **Context** here is slightly widened from that of working in private practice with Lucy. My reflection process took place because I wanted to give a case-study example of what I was writing about to do with the observer self. This book is meant to be relevant for practitioners across all modalities and, as it turned out, I came up with a list that could come from a range of theoretical approaches. I did not think of that in advance, though, it was only afterwards, when I was reflecting on the list that I noticed what I had done. I think this was an example of my knowing more than I could say at the time, and demonstrating my knowing in my doing, which is the point Schön is making in his book.
- The **Practitioner**. While 'Lucy' is a composite, I often work with clients who cannot make decisions, seemingly having given up their capacity to sense and feel for themselves because they were valued for giving way to others in their early lives. Many of them are women. While I often work with men who have also given up their capacity to sense and feel it is usually for a different reason – something about achievement and endurance. I noticed my own feminist values coming to the fore while I was writing the case study, and notice them again as I write this. I also recall how my own sense of self was lost in my early life – and I feel sad as I think of it. Working therapeutically with my clients, I draw on the gestalt theories that I learned in my main training, and that I still find so elegant, but I have other theories and approaches I can use. I learned them from my reading, personal and professional development activities (including therapy with practitioners from a range of modalities), and from my teaching.

Fundamentally, the question why do I know what I know as a therapist relates to my early life experience, culture, initial training, and subsequent learning and experience – the aspects of the Practitioner that are explored in earlier parts of this book.

ACTIVITY

Individual reflection

10.4 The suggestion for reflection from the previous section invited you to ask: What is your own process for choosing particular interventions? Perhaps allow your 'observing ego' to inform you as you work with your clients. Journal to explore how much of your decision-making process is associated with thoughts, feelings, body sensations or intuitions, or a balance of some or all of them.

If you have already done it, turn back to it in your journal. Otherwise, maybe you would like to do it now.

Refer to your piece of writing and wonder why you knew the answers you came up with. Were there any theoretical models you applied? Why did you happen to use those models?

Supervision

Here is where the 'dialogue between the external supervisor and the internal supervisor' (Casement, 1992: 32) takes place. Or is it? Casement acknowledges that while the external supervisor is present, maybe the internal supervisor is not yet sufficiently developed in the supervisee when he or she is only beginning to practise. Gilbert and Evans write:

> We recognize a distinction between training supervision and consultative supervision as is now beginning to be more widely honoured in the field of supervision (Carroll, 1996). The term 'training supervision' is used to describe the process of supervision of a psychotherapist during training. The tern 'consultative supervision' is used to refer to the process whereby an experienced and qualified practitioner seeks consultation with a peer or with a more experienced psychotherapist concerning client work.
>
> (2000: 3)

Hawkins and Shohet (2006: 60) also recognize that there is a difference in the function of supervision, depending on the stage the supervisee has reached. For the purposes of this discussion about competence and supervision, I will describe how the role of the supervisor differs in training supervision and consultative supervision. Although there are some functions that are performed during both stages, they might be approached differently. This section is relevant for both supervisor and supervisee, because it explores how they might work together to maintain competence. Supervision has such a strong influence on the supervisees' client work that the competence inherent in the supervisory relationship is likely to contribute to competence in the therapeutic relationship. Stoltenberg and Delworth observe:

> Pierce and Schauble (1970) found that trainees whose supervisors displayed high levels of empathy, regard, genuineness and concreteness also rated high in these qualities. Trainees with supervisors who had low levels of these attributes showed a decrease in these qualities.
>
> (1987: 153)

Training supervision

Casement says this of the supervisory role when the practitioner is at the beginning of training:

> Therefore, when a student therapist begins to work with training cases under supervision, the supervisor has a crucially important function in holding the student during the opening phase of clinical work – whilst he or she is learning to hold the patient analytically. The supervisor provides a form of control, making it safe for the therapist and patient to become analytically engaged, and helping a student to understand and to contain what is being presented by the patient. The foundations are laid down here for working independently later on.
>
> (1992: 32)

While Casement writes from an analytic perspective, it is probable that the necessity for trainees to feel securely held themselves, so that they can learn to hold their clients, would make sense across the different modalities. He implies that the role of the supervisor is to help the student develop a capacity to do for themselves what the supervisor is currently doing for them – to help in the development of the internal supervisor, or observer self.

Gilbert and Evans (2000: 48) have identified four phases in the development of the internal supervisor:

1   Learning to be inclusive without losing oneself in the client.
2   Learning to be fully present without losing sight of the other.
3   Holding both polarities albeit tentatively and sporadically.
4   Being able to move smoothly and consistently between self and other while simultaneously reflecting on self in relation to other and the process between.

How might a supervisor help a new practitioner to develop this capacity? Ryan recommends an approach to supervision (and being) that she describes as 'mindful': 'Mindful supervision encourages us to base our actions upon our real embodied experience' (2008: 72). She says about supervision, although it applies equally to therapy: 'When I stop to look at what is really going on: with me, the client and the space between then practice becomes an everyday miracle' (p. 70). Being mindful involves being present in the moment. Embodied presence can be achieved by grounding ourselves in our sensory experience: what we see, hear, feel in our bodies (smell and taste too, although these are less predominant in a therapy situation). Being embodied means taking focus away from the constant chatter in our minds, and becoming centred in our selves, to lose our minds and come to our senses, as Fritz Perls would have it. When we can quiet our minds, or even just take a step away from the constant noise in order to notice it, we can be in touch with our observer selves. The observer self can begin to become an internal supervisor.

Casement drew a distinction between an 'internalized supervisor' and an internal supervisor. It is unhelpful if a new practitioner 'swallows whole' what she or he learns from a supervisor. Ryan suggests that supervision, 'encourages us to make theories, maps and models for practice which are meaningful for us' (2008: 72). By working towards that end, both supervisee and supervisor will contribute towards the development of a sound internal supervisor. Carroll and Gilbert (2005: 35) offer a perspective on this process. Their three-stage model suggests that at the beginning, supervisees use their internal critics as supervisors. The next stage is where the internalized supervisor is formed. The final stage of the process is when the internal supervisor is fully developed.

Student therapists will almost certainly have more limits to their competence than more experienced practitioners. In my experience, they are also likely to be more self-conscious about their limitations, or else in denial of them to an extent. Negotiating a supervisory relationship that substantially frees a student from shame or arrogance is important because it is only then that competence can honestly be examined.

Every one of us will have limits to our competence of which we are not aware. Beginners are likely to have less awareness than more experienced practitioners. Supervisors may be very well aware of limits to competence that the trainee does not see. The supervisor then has to negotiate the delicate task of helping the trainee see the situation more clearly. Something that helps to make such a task more manageable for both participants is to discuss it at the outset of the supervision arrangement, and agree a way of dealing with it before it happens. It is also helpful if the supervisor can create an atmosphere that encourages 'being interested' about how and why situations arise, rather than believing there has to be a right or wrong way for them to happen. Students are often required to obtain a report from their supervisor to submit to their training provider as one of the criteria for successful completion of the stage they are in, or the course as a whole. They usually know the date by which the report is required. Completion of it can be a particular focus for exploring where a student feels they are in their learning, although it is likely that would be an ongoing discussion too.

Deficits to competence are likely to be made good as the student continues with training and client work. Supervisors may choose to take an educative role and help students understand a particularly relevant aspect of theory. They may also give students procedural information they do not have, for example, how to use CORE forms; or else suggest they seek information from an appropriate source, finding out what the suicide policy is in the agency where the student is placed for instance.

It is to be hoped that a situation in which a supervisor has grave concerns about a student which could not be resolved between them, would be a rare occurrence. Some training organizations have a procedure to follow in those circumstances, which is likely to be included in the documentation that is issued to supervisors. Although it would be a worst-case scenario, a training supervisor does usually have recourse to some other authority that can enforce any remedial action – which would most likely be that the student stops seeing clients temporarily, or may even be asked to leave the course.

Consultative supervision

My observation has been that the more experienced a practitioner becomes, the more willing they are to discuss the occasions when things go wrong. I have noticed this in myself in both consultative and peer supervision, with others in my supervision group, and with the more senior practitioners to whom I offer supervision.

The task is different from that in training supervision: the deficits in competence are likely to be fewer because of the additional training and experience qualified practitioners have. They are also likely to be more familiar with their own vulnerable areas of practice and so are watchful around them, and have strategies for dealing with them.

We all have limits to our competence. When a practitioner brings a situation which has felt like a breach of competence, a consultative supervisor will have a range of responses:

- The least interventionist response might be to offer reassurance, along the lines of 'no wonder you found it difficult to deal with, it's a very challenging situation, I think you did the best anyone could in the circumstances.' This kind of compassionate response from a fellow professional can both heal our vulnerabilities and strengthen our robustness for practice.
- A consultative supervisor might offer information like: 'when I had a client who was very patronizing, I gave him a copy of my CV...', give some explanation of theory or refer the supervisee to a relevant book or article. She or he may suggest training courses that might interest the supervisee.
- There may be a discussion of whether the situation is evoking something in the supervisee's own process. A brief exploration may take place within supervision, or it may be agreed that the supervisee needs to re-enter therapy. Supervisors are likely to have individual views about how the boundary between therapy and supervision is managed.

There are likely to be occasions when we move outside our levels of competence and are not aware of it. Supervisors may consider it part of their role to create opportunities to facilitate a widening of supervisees' awareness so that gaps can be acknowledged and addressed. I believe that this would be both supportive for supervisees and a contribution towards maintaining high standards for the profession as a whole. Individual supervisors will have ways of approaching this that are familiar from their particular theoretical orientation. Some possibilities are:

- Encouraging a brief discussion of the supervisee's current life circumstances, either as a 'check-in' at the beginning, or at some point during the session. If there are exceptional circumstances taking place, the consultative supervisor may then be especially vigilant to notice how client work might be affected if similar material is involved.

- Watching for communication that is 'out of tune'. For example, when the words are saying one thing, but the body process, or tone of voice is saying another.
- Encouraging creative approaches to supervision: using image and metaphor; objects such as shells or pebbles to depict individuals or situations.
- Exploring dreams supervisees might have about clients (or supervisors).

Where a consultative supervisor is gravely concerned about a supervisee's practice and the supervisee does not share that concern, then the context is likely to determine possibilities for taking further action. If the supervisee is connected with an organization either as an employee, or as a volunteer, then the supervisor could take the concerns to someone in a managerial role within it. The process may be different depending on the supervisor's relationship with the organization. The supervisor may be embedded in the organizational structures, or may be outside them, engaged in a limited contractual capacity. It is helpful if the appropriate person within the organization, with whom the supervisor would make contact in such circumstances, is identified when the supervision contract is being negotiated initially. If the supervisee works in independent private practice, then the only recourse might be to take the step of approaching the professional organization to which the supervisee belongs.

None of the courses of action that a supervisor might take if a supervisee refuses to listen to their concerns are easy choices. If they are to be avoided then perhaps it is important that supervisors continue to develop their 'authority, presence and impact' (Hawkins and Shohet, 2006: 128).

Peer supervision

More experienced practitioners may choose to meet together in pairs or groups to offer and receive supervision from each other. Where authority lies in this model is less clear than if there is a defined supervisor/supervisee relationship. Each participant may offer to the others involved the same approach to dealing with breaches of competence that a consultative supervisor would, in which case the discussion of that role in the previous section might apply equally to them. If peer supervision is the only supervision practitioners receive, it may be important to come to an agreement about how to deal with breaches of competence among those involved, so that a mechanism is in place.

Group supervision

Training, consultative and peer supervision can all take place in a group setting. In a training supervision context, the role of the supervisor would be to help participants begin to learn how to take a supervisory role with one another: combining the development of an internal supervisor with the capacity to participate in external supervision.

In consultative supervision, participants are generally encouraged to offer observations and feedback to one another, not only to receive them from the designated supervisor. The advantage to this is that more awareness can be gained from accessing all the different perspectives. The designated supervisor would probably assume main responsibility for dealing with group process but, again, this might be shared if group-members have the capacity, or it may be that it could be developed over time. In a peer supervision group, participants would take equal responsibility for dealing with group dynamics. Creating a climate where breaches to competence can be openly and compassionately discussed would be important whatever the supervision configuration. The responsibility for challenging a participant's practice where that is necessary, would be a helpful negotiation for any of them to undertake.

Supervising others

When I was training there were no dedicated supervision courses available, at least, if there were, news of them did not reach me. I learned about supervision in my training with Petruska Clarkson. She observed my work with others in the group and eventually told me I could supervise. So I did. By then I had experienced years and years of supervision and starting to offer it to others felt like a natural progression.

Casement writes:

> Here there are endless opportunities for therapists to re-examine their own work, when looking closely at the work of the person being supervised.

> (1992: 33)

Supervision of supervision has not been featured very prominently in professional journals in the past, although it is starting to be discussed as a specific approach currently. Writers who specialize in supervision, of course acknowledge the necessity for it (Gilbert and Evans, 2000; Hawkins and Shohet, 2006).

Here is my teacher's view of it:

> I personally do not see supervision of supervision as requiring an endlessly escalating developmental hierarchy ... Supervision is the space needed for reflecting on reflection. In my own experience it is the active involvement of colleagues in one's ongoing professional life, a drawing on resources and perspectives outside one's own world view, as well as the opportunity to contribute such vision, support and challenge to others.
>
> (Clarkson, 1998: 136)

So, it is not necessary for there to be a hierarchy with some sort of arch-supervisor sitting at the top of it. We can perform like a network, supporting others to maintain their competence, as they support us to maintain ours.

Conclusion

Networks of supervision can serve to support practitioners and maintain high levels of competence within the profession. Nevertheless, supervisors are likely to be the 'first-line' for dealing with breaches of competence. With goodwill and appropriate contractual arrangements in place, issues can be recognized and resolved. Situations that may be more problematic would include those where a supervisor may have concerns about a supervisee, or even feel critical of their work, and the supervisee does not believe the concern, or criticism is justified. There may be practical limits to a supervisor's authority in some contexts, particularly in independent private practice.

Hawkins and Shohet observe, 'Our experience has been that supervision can be a very important part of taking care of oneself' (2006: 5). The following chapter looks at self-care more widely.

The principle of:

Making good use of supervision

is added to the Competence Framework, so it becomes:

PRINCIPLES OF THE COMPETENCE FRAMEWORK

Cultivation the self in relationship
Recognizing the impact of difference
Acknowledging strengths and limitations of training
Understanding the nature of the client and possibilities for therapeutic relationship
Awareness of context
Identifying and remedying difficulties
Making good use of supervision

Chapter summary

The chapter included discussion of the following topics:

- Internal supervisor – development and practice of the observer self.
- Reflective practice – allowing what we learn from our work to come into awareness.
- Supervision: Training, Consultative, Peer, Group – a discussion of how the different configurations for supervision can be used to maintain competence, and how breaches can be dealt with.

Chapter 11

Highlighting personal self-care

Chapter outline

Understanding the care that a 'self' needs means defining what it is. The notion of 'self as story' offers the flexibility to reflect adequately on the experience of life. The self is embodied, and belongs in an interconnected world. The connection is with nature, as well as with other humans. An experience of 'mystery': spirituality, religion, the numinous is also important for the nourishment of the self.

Introduction

The self is what we use to do our job. It is formed by means of our early childhood relationships, as discussed in Chapter 3, and is honed and developed by our training, personal therapy and life experience, which is explored in Chapter 6. In the same chapter, the work of Orlinsky and Rønnestad (2009) describes how the self of the practitioner is developed through engagement with clients. We acknowledge the 'self-as-instrument' that comes in to play as we meet with our clients, supervisees and students, and the observer self that performs the role of internal supervisor (Chapter 10) as fundamental aspects of our work.

This chapter begins with exploring some of the different definitions of self, and arriving at an understanding of what it might mean for the purposes of this book. Possibilities for identifying and fulfilling the care needs of our selves are then discussed.

My self, your self, the self

There are many ways of talking about self. Probably every modality has its own particular way of defining it. As a gestaltist, I am very aware that the self can be construed as both structure and process.

The very concept of 'self' as conceived for the past several centuries (i.e. as an entity) lacks the depth and flexibility which we experience in our lives. The pioneers of psychotherapy intuited the inadequacy of a solid state model of self, and they introduced a class of metaphors which hinted at the radical mutability of what had previously been conceived of as sacred and inviolable. This was a step in the right direction, but the metaphors which Freud, Jung and others relied on to illuminate the idea of self did not go far enough in expressing its flexibility. Curiously, nearly all of the psychological metaphors related to the idea of 'self' have been visual: whether we're discussing Freudian 'ego-ideals', Jungian archetypal images of 'Self' or Rogerian 'self-images', the visual metaphor has long been dominant within our field. It's a theoretical advance from the time when self was considered entirely static, but a visual image still implies a kind of slow-to-change, almost-fixed picture of self – which is supposedly representative of our experience.

A 'self-story' by contrast, is a metaphor which suggests continuity *and* [italics in original] change – in dynamic proportion to one another.

(Roberts in Wheeler, 1998: 197)

As Roberts indicates, all theories of self are only metaphors, or stories; rudimentary and makeshift in comparison with the reality of being. Nevertheless, '[t]he story we tell ourselves about ourselves is a powerful psychological construct which is created in relationship and which exerts a profound influence on our experienced reality' (p. 196). So, while we can to a certain extent choose a metaphor, or story that has resonance for us, the one we do choose is likely to shape the way we make meaning about our selves. For the exploration of self-care to follow, I am proposing to define 'self' in a similar way to Roberts' concept of 'self-story':

[In] addition to the seemingly infinite flexibility of our self-story, there is an equally unmistakable constancy to it: it's somehow relatively stable and enduring, despite the fact that each day brings new scenarios, new characters, new possibilities.

(Roberts in Wheeler, 1998: 196)

REFLECTION POINTS

How does the modality in which you trained conceptualize the self? (Journal 5 minutes)

How do you experience your self? (Journal 10 minutes)

Care of the self

So far, self has been defined as both a structure which is consistent and recognizable over time, and a process, created in the present moment and with the potential to be created anew when circumstances change. Roberts' assertion that the self is formed in relationship is amply borne out by the theorists discussed in Chapter 3.

This is what Wilber has to say:

> [W]hen you say 'My self,' you draw a boundary line between what is you and what is not you ... The most common boundary line that individuals draw up or accept as valid is that of the skin-boundary surrounding the total organism. This seems to be a universally accepted self/not-self boundary line. Everything on the inside of that skin-boundary is 'not-me.' Something outside the skin-boundary may be 'mine' but it's not 'me'...
>
> If a boundary line *within* [italics in original] the organism seems strange to you, then let me ask, 'Do you feel you *are* a body, or do you feel you *have* a body?' Most individuals feel that they *have* a body, as if they owned or possessed it much as they would a car, a house or any other object ... Biologically there is not the least foundation for this dissociation or radical split between the mind and the body, the psyche and the soma, the ego and the flesh, but psychologically it is epidemic.
>
> (1979: 5–6)

This statement of Wilber emphasizes that the self is embodied. Rogers indicates the importance of 'the free experiencing of the actual sensory and visceral reactions of the organism' underlining that a person 'can *be* [italics in original] his [sic] experience with all its variety and sur-face contradiction, that he can formulate himself out of his experience, instead of trying to impose a formulation of self upon his experience, denying to awareness those elements which do not fit' (1967: 80). His view of what is often called the 'real self' certainly requires the involve-ment of a body.

Wilber has more to say about the boundary line that defines the self:

> The most interesting thing about this boundary line is that it can and frequently does shift. It can be re-drawn. In a sense, the person can re-map his [sic] soul and find in it territories he never thought possi-ble, attainable, or even desirable. As we have seen, the most radical re-mapping or shifting of the boundary line occurs in experiences of

the supreme identity, for here the person expands his self-identity boundary to include the entire universe.

(1979: 5)

Here, Wilber connects the self with trans-personal or spiritual dimensions. Individuals' relationships with the spiritual are often very personal. Here, I have no wish to impose any particular belief or values system, only to suggest that many of us will connect with a sense of there being something numinous about existence, whatever it looks like.

The nature of the self that emerges from these discussions is that it is relational, embodied and seeks meaning beyond the everyday (perhaps what Campbell called 'the reality-beyond-meaning' (2002:151)).

Who are my relations?

Everything is interconnected and the meaning derives from the total situation.

(Parlett, 1991: 71)

In the important article about Lewin's Field Theory from which this extract is taken, Parlett quotes Berman:

The view of nature which predominated in the West down to the eve of the scientific revolution was that of an enchanted world. Rocks, trees, rivers and clouds were all seen as wondrous, alive, and human beings felt at home in this environment. The cosmos, in short, was a place of belonging. A member of this cosmos was not an alienated observer of it but a direct participant in its drama. His [sic] personal destiny was bound up with its destiny, and this relationship gave meaning to his life. This type of consciousness – 'participating consciousness' – involved ... identification with one's surroundings and bespeaks a psychic wholeness that has long since passed from the scene.

(Berman, 1981: 16, in Parlett, 1991: 74)

This is in contrast to:

The story of the modern epoch, at least on the level of the mind, is one of progressive disenchantment ... scientific consciousness is alienated consciousness: there is no ecstatic merger with nature, but rather total separation from it. Subject and object are always seen in opposition to each other. I am not my experiences, and thus not part of the world around me.

(Berman, 1981:16, in Parlett, 1991:74)

Disconnection from our context, the Earth, has allowed humanity to make the choices that have led us to the point where we are talking about the possibility of her – and our – destruction. Feelings of loss for the 'wondrous, alive' world that our ancestors belonged to, and which some indigenous people still know, are probably so far out of our awareness in the west that we have forgotten to feel them. All that remains for many of us is the knowledge that being 'in nature' is restoring and uplifting in a profound way.

What is the individual's *natural relationship* [italics in original] to other people? Or is there a 'natural' relationship at all? There is. It is incorrect to assume that we 'construct' the way we relate to one another out of nothing at all – that there is no underlying order to the ways we can relate. Such an assumption is only possible if we radically dissociate ourselves from the rest of nature, where it is obvious that everything – including animals, inorganic matter, and energy – relates to everything else in complex but orderly ways.

(Roberts, 1999: 41)

While the 'wonder' may seem to have been lost, we can still connect to the inherent wisdom that surrounds us, and of which we are a part: 'By helping the client attend to her experiencing process, we enable her to access the intelligence of the field' (Roberts, 1999: 42). By attending to our own 'experiencing process' we can make that connection too. Gestaltists use what we call awareness to notice our experience. Other practitioners use the term 'Mindfulness'.

Basically 'mindfulness' is learning how to pay attention in the present moment without evaluation or judgement; it's using your conscious awareness and directing your attention to observe and *only* [italics in original] observe.

(Gilbert, 2010: 249)

Here again is reference to an observer self, similar to that which Casement described as being necessary for the internal supervisor. Cultivating that observer self can be as supportive to us in our lives as it is in our work.

As Siegel writes, 'Being fully present through mindful awareness training has been demonstrated to be a crucial factor in giving us resilience to face challenges that arise in our daily lives' (2010: 3).

Mindfulness is about being in the present. It is about being present in the present, rather than recalling the past or anticipating the future. In his book *The Spell of the Sensuous*, David Abram tells of his travels as an anthropologist, and as a sleight-of-hand magician, amongst indigenous peoples. He offers the following meditation:

> There is a useful exercise I devised … to keep myself from falling completely into the civilized oblivion of linear time. You are welcome to try it next time you are out of doors. I locate myself in a relatively open space – a low hill is particularly good, or a wide field. I relax a bit, take a few breaths, gaze around. Then I close my eyes, and let myself begin to feel the whole bulk of my past – the whole mass of events leading up to this very moment. And I call into awareness, as well, my whole future – all those projects and possibilities that lie waiting to be realized. I imagine this past and this future as two vast balloons of time, separated from each other like the bulbs of an hourglass, yet linked together at the single moment where I stand pondering them. And then, very slowly, I allow both of these immense bubbles of time to begin leaking their substance into this minute moment between them, into the present. Slowly, imperceptibly at first, the present moment begins to grow. Nourished by the leakage from the past and the future, the present moment swells in proportion as those other dimensions shrink. Soon it is very large, and the past and future have dwindled down to mere knots on the edge of this huge expanse. At this point I let the past and future dissolve entirely. And I open my eyes…
>
> (1997: 202)

Here are some other ways of healing the connection with the wider field:

- attend to the necessity of air, water and earth to sustain life;
- be interested in sustainability – make choices that benefit the whole;
- eat wholesome food, produced in sustainable ways;
- spend time at beautiful places: the seaside, mountains, forests, grasslands…;
- encourage wildlife;
- grow something, even herbs on a windowsill. Feel earth on your hands.

At home in body

Ways that help us be present to ourselves in the moment often involve connection with the breath, and with our senses. Breath is with us from the moment we enter the world until we die. It animates and provokes us – we use the word 'inspire' to mean both breathe in and stimulate. Attending to our breath helps us to reach a place of mindful awareness. It also connects us to everything else:

> What the plants are quietly breathing out, we animals are breathing in, what we breathe out the plants are breathing in. The air, we might say, is the soul of the visible landscape, the secret realm from whence all beings draw their nourishment. As the very mystery of the living present, [air] is the most intimate absence from whence the present presences, and thus is the key to the forgotten presence of the earth.
>
> (Abram, 1997: 226)

In his book, *The Feeling of What Happens: body, emotion and the making of consciousness*, Damasio writes, 'the organism is involved in relating to some object, and … the object in the relation is causing a change in the organism' (2000:133). As therapists, we understand that relating with other is fundamental to our experience. Yet how exactly do we relate with other? The only way it can happen is by means of our senses. Gestaltists sometimes refer to the senses as 'contact functions'. While it is a utilitarian description, it does reveal something of their nature and purpose that is important and often forgotten. Giving attention to our sensory reality can keep us embodied in the present, and alive to our experience. A reminder about the senses: sight, touch, hearing, smell and taste are the five senses to which people most often refer. In addition, we have what is called 'proprioception' – this is our sense of what is going on in the inside. Some meditation approaches use attention to the proprioceptive sense (noticing what is happening in the body) as a focus.

The new techniques in Neuroscience that are providing evidence for the effects of therapy, are also being used to show the benefit of yoga for alleviating depression, anxiety and PTSD, and to promote general wellbeing. They show how physical postures, breathing techniques and meditation cause beneficial changes to happen in the brain (Ryan, 2012).

Here are some body-care practices:

- Notice your breath. Tuning in to the breath is a quick way of returning to the self.

- Participate in a physical activity that is pleasurable for you: yoga, football, golf, swimming, walking, vigorous gardening, karate, running marathons, climbing etc.
- Rest. As much as your body needs.
- Enable wholesome sleep. Some people like to keep regular hours for going to sleep and waking up, finding a routine helpful.
- Laugh, cry, dance, sing…
- Touch another being.

Being creative

I have noticed that when they have reached a certain point in their healing and development work, people start to become creative. I have observed this in my self and also with clients. Nurturing our imaginative, generative aspects means that more of us is expressed in the world, and that has significance for our general wellbeing: 'The making of art is intoxicating, one of the great joys of life. In the creative process, as in falling in love, we contact our sweetness, longing, powerful attention, and profound thoughtfulness' (Zinker, 1978: 5).

Of course, therapy itself is creative. We can use the same techniques to replenish our selves that creative artists employ. Julia Cameron, author of *The Artist's Way*, writes:

> In order to create, we draw from our inner well. This inner well, an artistic reservoir, is ideally like a well-stocked trout pond. We've got big fish, little fish, fat fish, skinny fish – an abundance of artistic fish to fry. As artists, we must realize that we have to maintain this artistic ecosystem. If we don't give some attention to upkeep, our well is apt to become depleted, stagnant or blocked.
>
> (Cameron, 1992: 20)

REFLECTION POINT

Consider the metaphor of the trout pond. How well-stocked is your pond at the moment? When it needs replenishing, how does it fill up again?

Enjoying the creative works of others can be restorative. Listening to music, visiting a gallery, going to the theatre or reading a book can offer a refreshing new perspective.

Spiritual self

If organized religion is important for you, then it can mean a great deal. In our society people often claim to be spiritual rather than religious. This can be significant too. As humans, we find ourselves drawn to the numinous and ineffable, and gain sustenance from it.

Ways of being spiritual:

- Establish a meditation practice.
- Pray. Not necessarily to any particular being.
- Engage in ritual: gather as a family to eat together; light a candle while bathing; collect meaningful objects together in a specific place.
- Many people enjoy the idea of pilgrimage, visiting a place known to have particular significance: a church; standing stones; a holy well. I keep meeting people who either have made, or are intending a pilgrimage to Santiago de Compostela in Spain, which involves walking an ancient route, that can take many weeks to cover.

REFLECTION POINT

What is it that connects you to 'mystery', whatever that means for you?

Conclusion

In this chapter I have explored the nature of the self, with the aim of understanding the kind of care our selves might need. As individuals, each of us will have a balance of self-care needs, which is likely to depend on who we are, and where we are in our lives. Books like *The Resilient Practitioner* (2011) by Skovholt and Trotter-Mathison offer a range of activities for exploring personal self-care needs. A questionnaire devised by Roger Higgins, together with other resources, can be found on line at:

http://ebookbrowse.com/assessment-of-self-care-worksheet-roger-higgins-doc-d215753349

The final principle is added to the Competence Framework:

Nurturing and replenishing the self

The entire framework becomes:

PRINCIPLES OF THE COMPETENCE FRAMEWORK

Cultivation of the self in relationship

Recognizing the impact of difference

Acknowledging strengths and limitations of training

Understanding the nature of the client and possibilities for therapeutic relationship

Awareness of context

Identifying and remedying difficulties

Making good use of supervision

Nurturing and replenishing the self

Chapter summary

The self is embodied and relational, and open to being moved by the ineffable. The care that is required involves attention to the needs of the body within the wider environment. The self is nourished by creativity and connection with spirituality.

Conclusion

The self is at the centre of therapeutic practice. Understanding how the self has come to be formed is the way that each individual can define what competence means in their own practice. The self develops through early experience, including the influences of gender, race and culture, sexuality, ability and disability, and class. It is refined by professional training, personal therapy and in day-to-day client work. The self is embodied, inter-dependent with other beings and the wider environment, and attracted towards the sacred, however that is construed.

Competence is distinct from effectiveness. The nature of therapeutic work means that practitioners need to be able to withstand relationship ruptures, 'mistakes' and uncertainty. Nissen-Lie, Monsen, Ulleberg and Rønnestad (2012) have identified that what they call Professional Self Doubt has a positive effect on outcomes for clients. It seems that the less sure a practitioner is of his or her effectiveness, the more effective he or she is likely to be. How, then, can competence be established and maintained? I believe that competence emerges from experience, training and being embedded in a professional structure. Singly, we are susceptible to being swept along by the powerful dynamics that take place in the therapeutic encounter. Together, we can provide solid frameworks to hold our selves, and our clients, supervisees and students.

This book has been an attempt to offer one such framework. The Competence Framework has three Elements and Eight Principles:

ELEMENTS OF THE COMPETENCE FRAMEWORK

- Practitioner
- Client
- Context

These three elements are meant to offer a brief and accessible way of making decisions that support competent practice with clients in the intensity of moment-by-moment therapeutic work. They inform the observer self that performs the role of internal supervisor (see Part II, Chapter 10). They offer a method for exploring situations where things might have gone awry (as demonstrated in Part I, Chapter 2).

The eight principles are a fuller statement of the values that underlie competent practice and may be used as for personal reflection and in Supervision.

PRINCIPLES OF THE COMPETENCE FRAMEWORK

Cultivation the self in relationship

Recognizing the impact of difference

Acknowledging strengths and limitations of training

Understanding the nature of the client and possibilities for therapeutic relationship

Awareness of context

Identifying and remedying difficulties

Making good use of supervision

Nurturing and replenishing the self

All of us have both powerful abilities, and limitations that make us vulnerable. If, as a profession, we can celebrate our abilities and be compassionate towards our limitations, we will offer a service that has true worth both for our clients, and the wider community.

References

Abram, J. (1997) *The Spell of the Sensuous.* New York: Vintage.

Aitken, F. and Coupe, A. (2006) *Difference and Diversity in Counselling: Contemporary Psychodynamic Perspectives.* Wheeler, S. (ed.). Basingstoke: Palgrave Macmillan.

American Psychiatric Association (2013) *Diagnostic and Statistical Manual of Mental Disorders.* Fifth Edition. Arlington, VA: American Psychiatric Publishing.

BACP (2010) *Ethical Framework for Good Practice in Counselling and Psychotherapy.* Lutterworth, UK: BACP.

Bager-Charlson, S. (2010) *Reflective Practice in Counselling and Psychotherapy.* Exeter: Learning Matters.

Bager-Charlson, S. (2012) *Personal Development in Counselling and Psychotherapy.* London: Sage.

Barden, N. (2006) *Difference and Diversity in Counselling: Contemporary Psychodynamic Perspectives.* Wheeler, S. (ed.). Basingstoke: Palgrave Macmillan.

Basch, M. (1988) *Understanding Psychotherapy.* New York: Basic Books.

Berman, J.S. and Norton, N.C. (1985) Does Professional Training Make Therapists more Effective? *Psychological Bulletin.* 98: 401–7.

Bond, T. (2010) *Standards and Ethics for Counselling in Action.* Third Edition. London: Sage.

Bond, T. and Jenkins, P. (2009) BACP Information Sheet G1: *Access to Records of Counselling and Psychotherapy.* Lutterworth, UK: BACP.

Brayne, M. (2007) Climate Change and a Couple of Needy Clients. *Therapy Today.* 18(10): 4–7.

Büber, M. (1958/1984) *I and Thou.* Edinburgh: T. & T. Clark.

Cameron, J. (1992) *The Artist's Way.* New York: Tarcher Putnam.

Campbell, J. (2002) *Flight of the Wild Gander.* Novato, CA: New World Library.

Carroll, M. and Gilbert, M.C. (2005) *On Being a Supervisee.* London: Vukani.

Casement, P. (1992) *On Learning from the Patient.* London: Routledge.

Clarkson, P. (1995) *The Therapeutic Relationship.* London: Whurr.

Clarkson, P. (1998) *Supervision: Psychoanalytic and Jungian Perspectives.* London: Whurr.

Clarkson, P. and Mackewn, J. (1993) *Fritz Perls.* London: Sage.

Coleridge, L. (2010) BACP Information Sheet P12: *Making Notes and Records of Counselling and Psychotherapy.* Lutterworth, UK: BACP.

Damasio, A. (2000) *The Feeling of What Happens.* London: Vintage.

Daniel, J. (2009) The Gay Cure. *Therapy Today.* 20(8): 10–12.

D'Ardenne, P. and Mahtani, A. (1999) *Transcultural Counselling in Action.* Second Edition. London: Sage.

Davies, D. and Neal, C. (eds) (1996) *Pink Therapy.* Buckinghamshire: Oxford University Press.

Despenser, S. (2008) Have you Made a Clinical Will? *Therapy Today.* 19(7): 31–3.

Dryden, W. (ed.) (1991) *Individual Therapy: A Handbook.* Buckinghamshire: Open University Press.

Erault, M. (2006) *Developing Professional Knowledge and Competence.* Abingdon, UK: RoutledgeFalmer.

Erikson, E. (1965) *Childhood and Society.* Harmondsworth: Penguin.

Freud, S. (1905) *Three Essays on the Theory of Sexuality.* Penguin Freud Library Volume 7. London: Penguin.

Freud, S. (1905a) 'On psychotherapy'. In J. Strachey (ed.), *The Standard Edition of the Complete Psychological Works of Sigmund Freud, Volume 7.* London: Hogarth.

Gilbert, M.C. and Evans, K. (2000) *Psychotherapy Supervision: An Integrative Approach to Psychotherapy Supervision.* Maidenhead, UK: Open University Press.

Gilbert, P. (2010) *The Compassionate Mind.* London: Constable.

Gilligan, C. (1993) *In a Different Voice.* Cambridge, MA: Harvard University Press.

Guntrip, H. (1968) *Schizoid Phenomena, Object Relations and the Self.* London: Hogarth Press.

Hawkins, P. and Shohet, R. (2006) *Supervision in the Helping Professions.* Third Edition. Buckinghamshire: Open University Press.

Hillman, J. and Ventura, M. (1993) *We've Had a Hundred Years of Psychotherapy and the World's Getting Worse.* San Francisco, CA: Harper.

Isaac, M. (2006) *Difference and Diversity in Counselling: Contemporary Psychodynamic Perspectives.* Wheeler, S. (ed.). Basingstoke: Palgrave Macmillan.

Jackson, C. (2012) Growing Old Happily. *Therapy Today.* 23(9): 6–7.

Jacobs, M. (2004) *Psychodynamic Counselling in Action.* Third Edition. London: Sage.

Joyce, P. and Sills, C. (2010) *Skills in Gestalt Counselling and Psychotherapy.* Second Edition. London: Sage.

Jung, C.G. (1917) 'The psychology of the unconscious'. In H. Read, M. Fordham and G. Adler (eds), *The Collected Works of C.G. Jung, Volume 7.* London: Routledge and Kegan Paul.

Kapadia, M. (2008) Adapting to Difference: The Hairdryer Theory. *Therapy Today*. 19(6): 16–20.

Kareem, J. and Littlewood, R. (eds) (2000) *Intercultural Therapy*. Second Edition. Oxford: Blackwell.

Kohut, H. (1984) *How Does Analysis Cure?* London: The University of Chicago Press.

Lago, C. (2006) *Race, Culture and Counselling*. Second Edition. Maidenhead, UK: Open University Press.

Lewin, K. (1952) *Field Theory in Social Science*. London: Tavistock.

Likierman, M. (2001) *Melanie Klein: Her Work in Context*. London: Continuum.

Littlewood, R. and Lipsedge, M. (1989) *Aliens and Alienists: Ethnic Minorities and Psychiatry*. Second Edition. London: Unwin Hyman.

Macy, J. (2007) Gratitude: Where Healing the Earth Begins. *Shambhala Sun*. November: 48–51.

Miller, A. (1995) *The Drama of Being a Child* (tr. Ruth Ward). Revised Edition. London: Virago.

Nissen-Lie, H., Monsen, J.T., Ulleberg, P. and Rønnestad, M.H. (2012) Psychotherapists' Self-reports of their Interpersonal Functioning and Difficulties in Practice as Predictors of Patient Outcome. *Psychotherapy Research. 1-19*. iFirst Article. Routledge.

Ogden, T. (1992) The Dialectically Constituted/Decentered Subject of Psychoanalysis. II: The Contributions of Klein and Winnicott. *International Journal of Psychoanalysis*. 73: 613–26.

Orlinsky, D.E. and Rønnestad, M.H. (2009) *How Psychotherapists Develop*. Washington, DC: American Psychological Association.

Panskepp, J. (2006) 'The core emotional systems of the mammalian brain: The fundamental substrates of human emotions'. In J. Corrigall, H. Payne and H. Wilkinson (eds), *About a Body: Working with the Embodied Mind in Psychotherapy*. Hove: Routledge.

Parlett, M. (1991) Reflections on Field Theory. *British Gestalt Journal*. 1(2): 69–81.

Peden, A. (2010) BACP Information Sheet G18: *Recognising and Acting on Child Sexual Abuse*. Lutterworth, UK: BACP.

Perls, F. (1992, originally published 1947) *Ego, Hunger and Aggression*. New York: Gestalt Journal Press.

Perls, F., Hefferline, R. and Goodman, P. (1951) *Gestalt Therapy: Excitement and Growth in the Human Personality*. London: Souvenir Press.

Reeve, D. (2000) Oppression within the Counselling Room. *Disability and Society*. 15(4): 669–82.

Roberts, A. (1999) The Field Talks Back. *British Gestalt Journal*. 8(1): 35–46.

Rogers, C. (1967) *On Becoming a Person*. London: Constable.

Ross, A. (2006) *Difference and Diversity in Counselling: Contemporary Psychodynamic Perspectives*. Wheeler, S. (ed.). Basingstoke: Palgrave Macmillan.

Roth, T. (2010) BACP Information Sheet R4: *Using Measures and Thinking about Outcomes*. Lutterworth, UK: BACP.

Rowan, J. (2005) *The Future of Training in Psychotherapy and Counselling*. Hove: Routledge.

Russell, M. and Simanowitz, V. (2013) Retirement or Renaissance? *Therapy Today*. 24(2): 15–18.

Ryan, J. (2012) Yoga for the Mind. *Therapy Today*. 23: 8.

Ryan, S. (2008) *Passionate Supervision* (ed. R. Shohet). London: Jessica Kingsley.

Ryde, J. (2009) *Being White in the Helping Professions*. London: Jessica Kingsley.

Sanders, P. (2009) Politics and Therapy. *Therapy Today*. 20(2): 17–19.

Scaife, J. (2010) *Supervising the Reflective Practitioner*. Hove: Routledge.

Schön, D. (1991) *The Reflective Practioner*. Farnham, UK: Ashgate.

Sedgwick, D. (2004) *The Wounded Healer: Counter-Transference from a Jungian Perspective*. London: Routledge.

Segal, J. (2006) *Difference and Diversity in Counselling: Contemporary Psychodynamic Perspectives*. Wheeler, S. (ed.). Basingstoke: Palgrave Macmillan.

Siegel, D.J. (2010) *The Mindful Therapist*. New York: Norton.

Skovholt, T. and Trotter-Mathison, M. (2011)*The Resilient Practitioner: Burnout Prevention and Self-care Strategies for Counselors, Therapists, Teachers and Health Professionals*. Second Edition. Abingdon, UK: Routledge.

Stern, D.N. (1985) *The Interpersonal World of the Infant*. New York: Basic Books.

Stolorow, R.D. and Atwood, G. E. (2002) *Contexts of Being: The Intersubjective Foundations of Psychological Life*. New Jersey: The Analytic Press.

Stoltenberg, C.D. and Delworth, U. (1987) *Supervising Counselors and Therapists: A Developmental Approach*. San Francisco, CA: Jossey-Bass.

Sue, D.W. and Sue, D. (1990) *Counselling the Culturally Different*. Second Edition. New York: John Wiley.

Sugg, S. (2011) Retirement: When is it Time to Stop? *Therapy Today*. 22(7): 17–19.

Teicholz, J.G. (2001) *Kohut, Loewald and the Postmoderns*. Hillsdale, NJ: The Analytic Press.

Thierault, A. and Gazzola, N. (2008) Feelings of Incompetence among Experienced Clinicians: A Substantive Theory. *European Journal for Qualitative Research in Psychotherapy*. Available: http://www.europeanresearchjournal.com (accessed 19 November 2012).

Tolan, J. (2012) *Skills in Person-centred Counselling and Psychotherapy*. Second Edition. London: Sage.

Totton, N. (2011) Wild Therapy. *Therapy Today*. 22(2): 10–14.

Walley, S. (2010) BACP Information Sheet P17: *Making Referrals*. Lutterworth, UK: BACP.

Wellington, H. (2006) *Difference and Diversity in Counselling: Contemporary Psychodynamic Perspectives.* Wheeler, S. (ed.). Basingstoke: Palgrave Macmillan.

Wheeler, G. (1998) *Gestalt Reconsidered: A New Approach to Contact and Resistance.* Cambridge, MA: GICpress.

Wheeler, S. (ed.) (2006) *Difference and Diversity in Counselling: Contemporary Psychodynamic Perspectives.* Basingstoke: Palgrave Macmillan.

White, A. (2011) There by the Grace of … *Therapy Today.* 22(5): 10–14.

Wilber, K. (1979) *No Boundary.* Boston: Shambhala.

Winnicott, D.W. (1951) Transitional Objects and Transitional Phenomena. In *Collected Papers: Through Paediatrics to Psycho-analysis.* New York: Basic Books (1975).

Winnicott, D.W. (1958) *Collected Papers: Through Paediatrics to Psycho-analysis.* London: Hogarth Press.

Winnicott, D.W. (1965) *The Maturational Processes and the Facilitating Environment, Studies in the Theory of Emotional Development.* London: Hogarth Press.

Yalom, J.D. (1991) *Love's Executioner and other Tales of Psychotherapy.* London: Penguin Books.

Zinker, J. (1978) *Creative Process in Gestalt Therapy.* New York: Vintage Books.

Index